AUTHOR

Dr Krishna Goel

BSc, MBBS, MD, FRCP (Lond, Edin & Glasg), FRCPCH (Hon)
Formerly Senior Lecturer in Child Health, University of Glasgow
&
Consultant Paediatrician
Royal Hospital for Sick Children, Yorkhill, Glasgow, Scotland, UK
(Currently at the Queen Elizabeth University Hospital,
ROYAL HOSPITAL for CHILDREN, Glasgow, G51 4TF)

ABOUT THE AUTHOR

Dr Krishna Goel has lived in Scotland for five decades after emigrating from India in
1965. He studied medicine in India and obtained further higher medical qualifications
in Glasgow, Scotland. He worked as a Consultant Paediatrician, specialising in
Paediatric Rheumatology for many years at Scotland's prestigious Royal Hospital for
Sick Children, Yorkhill, Glasgow. He was one of the founder directors of the Children's
Hospice Association Scotland (CHAS), and a former Trustee of Yorkhill Children's
Trust, the Ronald McDonald House Charities, Glasgow and Eredine Christian Trust.
He has co-authored textbooks on paediatrics and recently published a book, *The
Plants of The Bible and their Medicinal Properties*. He is married to Joyce Goel, is now
retired and lives in Helensburgh, Argyll & Bute, Scotland.

Published 2016

From Rt Hon Nicola Sturgeon MSP
First Minister of Scotland

❝I am hugely proud that, for a small country, Scotland has contributed so much to the world. From the entrepreneurial spark of Andrew Carnegie to the conservationism of John Muir, our nation has gifted the world with innovative, gusty and brave men and women who have been trailblazers in all walks of life.

Indeed, without our inventive spark, there would be no TVs, no telephones, no fridges, and – of course - no whisky!

But nowhere is the spirit of Scotland more evident than in its people, and visitors to our country can be guaranteed that the people they meet and the welcome they receive will leave a lasting impression. I am incredibly proud to lead a nation of such warm, determined, driven and good-humoured people, whose hard work has benefitted nations right across the globe - and *Some Great Scots* by Doctor Krishna Goel is a valuable addition to our understanding of how our country has helped shape the modern world.❞

FOREWORD

Scotland is a small, but remarkable country. It has beautiful landscapes, mountains and lochs, historic towns and cities, world-renowned universities, and a distinctive history and culture. Most of all, however, its people have contributed enormously to ideas and inventions which have changed the world.

This book, in a concise way, sets out the story of these great Scots, and these men and women cover all aspects of human endeavour. For example, in literature, in additions to the legends of Burns, Scott and Stevenson, we have a host of modern writers. In the arts there are the Glasgow Boys and linked to architecture with Charles Rennie MacIntosh. In science and technology there are numerous examples, from the invention of the telephone and television to Dolly the Sheep. In medicine there have been discoveries in anaesthesia, antisepsis and antibiotics to name but three. The whole Enlightenment movement in the 18th century began in Scotland and is linked to names such as Adam Smith and David Hume. Physicists, chemists and mathematicians abound. The first youth movement in the world, The Boy's Brigade, began in Scotland through the efforts of William Smith and is now worldwide. Scotland has also been the birthplace of political movements and of politicians who have changed our thinking. But you need to read the book to get the full range of people and their contributions.

The question is why did Scotland give birth to a wide range of people with so many ideas? To some extent this relates to strong national education programmes and the encouragement to learn and to question. Perhaps it was also associated with the culture of the country, post-reformation, with its emphasis on doing good works, and indeed on working hard. It was possible for people of lowly birth to reach the highest levels and to contribute to a wider world and society. Then there is the importance of freedom of speech and the ability to debate difficult issues, to challenge conventional wisdom, and to change things for the better.

And do these trends continue? Can, and does, Scotland still contribute to the world in the way that is so obvious in the past? The answer of course, is yes, and if we ever gave up the quest for new ideas and inventions it would be bad for Scotland. This book shows just how much we have contributed and can continue to do so in so many fields; literature and the arts, science and medicine, the social sciences and philosophy. It also challenges us to continue that process and keep Scotland at the leading edge of ideas and change. The book will provide the inspiration for the Great Scots of the future; there are many more great Scots to come!

Sir Kenneth C Calman
Chancellor
University of Glasgow

PREFACE

Scotland is not just a country with spectacular scenery comprising lochs, glens, hills, mountains and beautiful landscapes. It is much more than that. For such a small nation Scotland has produced an amazing number of outstanding men and women. By their inventions, discoveries and writings they changed the world for the better. Indeed a remarkable achievement for Scotland.

Why did I embark on the project of writing this book? The answer is simple. Recently I asked a number of people resident in Scotland from varied backgrounds to name ten famous Scots. Surprisingly, most struggled to get to a double-digit figure. That is why. There is no agreed definition of Scottish; obviously one cannot base it on accent. The most obvious test of being Scottish is having been born in Scotland. *In this book the term 'Scots' refers to people who were born in Scotland, but also to those born outside of Scotland who spent a significant time living in the country and identified with a Scottish ancestry. Only a handful of people included are naturalised Scots.*

I hope that the reader will find this book interesting and informative. I also hope they may wish to use the material to educate and inform children. It can be enjoyed by newcomers to Scotland and by those who have lived there all their lives and thus be proud of their nationality and realise what a **MAGNIFICENT HERITAGE** they have.

Finally, the book should not be regarded as an attempt to produce a definitive account of all Great Scots. This is not a scholarly study of the role of Scots on the national and international stage.

CONTENTS

Some Great Scots comprise philosophers, inventors, physicians and surgeons, poets, novelists, artists, explorers, architects, civil engineers and builders, industrialists, philanthropists, economists, naturalists, biographers, Christian missionaries, entertainers, musicians, singers, statesman, lexicographers, geographers, explorers, plant hunters and pioneers in the fields of research that created the Dolly the sheep, the world's first cloned mammal.

SECTION A:
The names on the list are in alphabetical order (by SURNAME):

30. **Keir Hardie:** Socialist, Founder of the Independent Labour Party, Forerunner of the British Labour Party (1856-1915)
31. **Elsie Maud Inglis:** Instrumental in Advancing the Cause of Women (1864-1917)
32. **William Jardine:** Businessman (1784-1843) and **James Matheson** (1796-1878)
33. **John Knox:** Father of Presbyterianism, Instrumental in Protestant Reformation in Scotland (1512-1572)
34. **Sir Thomas Lipton:** Grocer (1850-1931)
35. **James Lind:** Found Cure for Scurvy (1716-1794)
36. **Eric Liddell:** Christian Missionary and Olympic Gold Medallist (1902-1945)
37. **Lord Lister:** Introduced Antiseptic Techniques (1827-1012)
38. **David Livingstone:** Christian Missionary and Explorer (1813 – 1873)
39. **Kirkpatrick Macmillan:** The Bicycle (1813-1873)
40. **Charles Macintosh:** Dyes and Rubber –The Raincoat (1766-1843)
41. **William Murdoch:** Gas Lighting (1754-1839)
42. **James Clerk Maxwell:** The Physicist (1831-1879)
43. **Andrew Barron Murray:** Tennis Player (1987-)
44. **John Louden McAdam:** Road Builder (1756-1836)
45. **Charles Rennie Macintosh:** Architect (1868-1928)
46. **Sir William McEwen:** Pioneer of Brain Surgery, Bone Graft Surgery and Thoracic Surgery (1848-1924)
47. **John Muir:** Naturalist and Conservationist (1838-1914)
48. **James Ramsay MacDonald:** Prime Minister (Labour, from 1929 to 1935, 1924 to 1924): (1866-1937)
49. **John Napier:** Invented Logarithm Tables (1550-1617)
50. **Sir William Ramsay:** Chemist Discovered Krypton, Argon, Neon, Xenon, and Helium. Recipient of Nobel Prize in 1904. (1852-1916)
51. **J K Rowling:** Author-Harry Potter (1965-)
52. **Alex Salmond:** First Nationalist to Lead the Devolved Scottish Government (1954-)
53. **Sir James Young Simpson:** Invented Chloroform General Anaesthetic (1811-1870)
54. **Sir Walter Scott:** Historical Novelist, Poet and Playwright (1771-1832)
55. **Mary Slessor:** Christian Missionary (1848-1915)
56. **Adam Smith:** Economist (1723-1790)
57. **John Smith:** Statesman (1938-1994)
58. **Robert Louis Stevenson:** Novelist and Poet (1850-1894)
59. **Jackie Stewart:** Professional Motor Racing Driver (1939-)
60. **William Alexander Smith:** Founder of Boys' Brigade (1854-1914)
61. **Nicola Sturgeon:** First Minister of Scotland (1970-)
62. **Thomas Telford:** Civil Engineer and Architect (1757-1834)
63. **William Thomson-Lord Kelvin:** Scientist (1824-1907)
64. **Sir James Young:** Paraffin Man (1811-1883)
65. **James Watt:** The Steam Engine (1736-1819)
66. **Sir Robert William-Watt:** Scientist, Developed Radar (1892-1973)
67. **Tom Weir:** Naturalist and Explorer (1914-2006)
68. **William Wallace:** Freedom Fighter (c. 1270-1305)

SECTION B:
OTHER GREAT SCOTS categorised according to SURNAME, (See table):

SECTION C:
SCOTTISH WWI HEROINES

SECTION D:
SCOTTISH PAINTERS:
(A)   THE GLASGOW BOYS:

1.   Joseph Crawhall
2.   Thomas Millie Dow
3.   David Gauld
4.   Sir James Guthrie
5.   James Whitelaw Hamilton
6.   George Henry
7.   Edward Atkinson Hornel
8.   William Kennedy
9.   Sir John Lavery
10. Alexander Mann
11. Charles Hodge Mackie
12. Thomas McEwan
13. William York Macgregor
14. Bessie McNicol
15. Arthur Melville
16. James Paterson
17. Alexander Roche
18. Macaulay Stevenson
19. Edward Arthur Walton
20. Closely associated with the Glasgow School of Art at various times were: J.E. Christie, J.S. Park, Sir George Pirie and Sir William MacTaggart

(B)   The NEWGLASGOW BOYS: (1983-1997)
• Adrian Wiszniewski
• Steven Campbell
• Ken Currie
• Peter Howson

(C)   SCOTTISH COLOURISTS: (1920 – 1930)
• Samuel Peploe
• Francis Cadell
• Leslie Hunter
• J.D. Fergusson

SECTION E:
Some of the 120 Scottish Plant Hunters:

1.   David Douglas
2.   James Drummond
3.   John Fraser
4.   George Forrest
5.   Robert Fortune
6.   Joseph Hooker
7.   David Lyall
8.   Francis Masson
9.   Archibald Menzies
10. George Sherriff
11. Thomas Thomson
12. Euan Cox, Peter Cox, Kenneth Cox
13. George Don

SECTION F:
SCOTLAND A PIONEER:
• The Game of Golf (Since the 15th century)
• Dolly the Cloned Sheep (1996-2003)

1. ## JOHN LOGIE BAIRD (1888 - 1946)

    ### KEY POINTS:

    - Born in Helensburgh, Argyll and Bute.
    - Studied Electrical Engineering in Glasgow.
    - On 26th January 1926, Baird gave the world's first public demonstration of true television to a group of about 50 scientists.
    - Set up the Baird Television Development Company. In 1928 was the first to demonstrate transmission between London and New York and the first transmission to a ship in the mid-Atlantic.
    - In 1928, he demonstrated the world's first colour television transmission. In 1944, two years before his death, he demonstrated a 600 line/high definition electronic colour television system. Baird looked forward to a great upsurge in the use of colour television after the War, but he did not live to see it.
    - Baird gave the world its greatest communications tool.
    - He died on June 14th, 1946, after suffering a stroke. He is buried in Helensburgh cemetery.
    - See figure 1

Figure 1: Monument to John Logie Baird at the promenade, Helensburgh, Argyll

2. Sir JAMES MATTHEW BARRIE (1860 – 1937)

KEY POINTS:

- Born in Kirriemuir, Angus.
- Novelist, playwright.
- Barrie is most famous for the play Peter Pan, or the boy who wouldn't grow up. Peter Pan, one of the greatest of 20th century myths was a work of art, unlike anything written previously. In Peter Pan, the distillation of years of thought, his immense artistic gift was displayed at its best.
- The eldest of the Darling children is WENDY. The Darling children fly away with PETER to Never-land or Never Never-land.
- It was revealed, in a late 19th century study of Barrie, that his mother – who greatly admired her son's work- nevertheless preferred the stories of Robert Louis Stevenson!
- He was Rector of the University of St. Andrews and Chancellor of Edinburgh University. He was knighted in 1913 and awarded the Order of Merit.
- His philanthropy went far beyond the valuable gift of the royalties from Peter Pan to the Great Ormond Street Hospital, London. In addition to many anonymous charitable gifts, he spent large amounts of his time writing plays and sketches for fund-raising.
- He died of pneumonia, aged 77 years.
- See figures: 2(a) and (b)

Figure 2(a): Birthplace of Sir James Matthew Barrie (centre, with hat).
(Courtesy of Angus Archives, Copyright Angus Council)

Figure 2(b): Peter Pan Children
(Illustrated by Duncan Galbraith, Tayinloan, Argyll)

3.   Lord ARTHUR JAMES BALFOUR (1848 – 1930)

KEY POINTS:

Figure 3: Lord Arthur Balfour

- A Conservative from East Lothian.
- Scottish-born Prime Minister. (Conservative from 1902 to 1905).
- The Balfour Declaration led to the CREATION of the STATE of ISRAEL.
- One of the most controversial decisions in foreign policy, because it sowed some of the seeds of the continuing conflict in the Middle East.
- He said: "I am more or less happy when being praised, not very comfortable when being abused, but I have moments of uneasiness when being explained".
- See figure 3

4.   HENRY BELL (1767 – 1830)

KEY POINTS:

- Born in Torphichen near Linlithgow in 1767.
- Played a prominent part in developing steamships.
- In 1808, he moved to Helensburgh where his wife ran the Baths Inn.
- Launched his boat The Comet on the River Clyde in January, 1812.
- The Comet was the first European Steamship in service – followed by the paddle steamers, Columba and Waverley.
- The Comet was in service until 1820, when it sank off the Western Isles.
- Became Lord Provost of Helensburgh.
- Henry Bell died in Helensburgh on 14th November, 1830.
- See figures: 4 (a) & (b)

Figure 4 (a): Memorial to Henry Bell in Rhu & Shandon Parish Church graveyard
(Photograph: Andrew M Nicholson, Rhu, Arygll)

Figure 4 (b): The Comet off Craigendoran
(Painting by Neil Macleod, Helensburgh, Argyll)

5.   ALEXANDER GRAHAM BELL (1847 – 1922)

KEY POINTS:

- Alexander Graham Bell was born in Edinburgh.
- Became interested in the transmission of speech along electric wires. Thus discovered how sound could be converted into electricity, sent long distances by wire, and converted back into sound.
- On 10th March 1876, Bell gave the first public demonstration of his telephone.
- In 1877, the Bell Telephone Company was established.
- He "taught the deaf to speak".
- The Royal Bank of Scotland celebrated his birth by issuing a £1 banknote in 1997. It was the first banknote in the EU to carry a hologram.
- Bell is remembered by fans of 1970s pop music: 'Alexander Graham Bell' was a hit for the Glam Rock group Sweet in 1971.
- Alexander Graham Bell died aged 75. All the telephones in the USA and Canada were silent for a minute as a mark of respect.
- See figures: 5(a) and (b)

Figure 5 (a):
BT Domestic Telephone

Figure 5 (b): The features on this banknote include: Alexander Graham Bell's portrait and name, a wave signal for "telephone" and a schematic drawing of a receiver. Also included are Mrs Bell (who was deaf) and representations of sign language and the phonetic alphabet developed by Bell's father. Birds and sheep, which helped him to understand genetics and geometric shapes, are shown to illustrate other scientific pursuits that occupied Bell.
(Courtesy The Royal Bank of Scotland)

6.   Sir JAMES BLACK (1924 – 2010)

KEY POINTS:

- James Whyte Black was the son of a coalmine manager from Fife.
- Studied medicine at St Andrews University.
- In 1964 he invented the drug Propranolol – commonly referred as a beta–blocker to treat hypertension and heart disease. Propranolol revolutionised heart treatment and is considered one of the most important contributions to clinical medicine and pharmacology of the 20th century.
- He also invented a drug which would prevent the hormone, histamine, from secreting gastric acid with a blocker H2 receptor. It is the acid that irritates the lining of the stomach which causes the pain, thus healing ulcers without surgery.
- In 1988, he was awarded the Nobel Prize for Physiology of Medicine.
- See figure 6

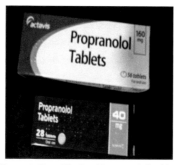

Figure 6: Beta-blocker (Propranolol tablets)

7. ROBERT BURNS (1759 – 1796)

KEY POINTS:

- Born in Alloway, Ayr.
- Burns was Scotland's most feted literary figure and was a man of his time. He is a poet for all moods, seasons and occasions. First collection of poems published in 1786. His poems and songs such as: *A Red Red Rose*; *A Man For A' That*; *Tam O' Shanter*; *To a Mouse* and other poems are famous. His works ranged from love lyrics to savage satire (*Holy Willie's Prayer*). His poems were translated into Russian and he featured on a Soviet stamp.
- He is not just Scotland's National Bard; his works are read and admired throughout the world.
- There is no other literary figure in whose name and on whose birthday (25th January), thousands of people across the world enjoy a ceremonial meal – the Burns Supper.
- In 1971, Clydesdale Bank introduced a portrait of Robert Burns on the front of the £5 banknote, in the Famous Scots Series.
- Despite-or perhaps because of-his poetic gift, Burns possessed a mercurial temperament which often left his affairs, both personal and professional, in a state of serious disarray. His life was both blighted and shortened by his apparent failure to understand and come to terms with his own nature.
- Robert Burns died in 1796, aged only 37.
- See figures:7 (a), (b), (c), (d), (e) & (f)

Figure 7 (a):
Monument to Robert Burns in Dumfries
(Photograph: Helen Braidwood, Dumfries)

Figure 7 (b):
Burns Statue in Ayr
(Photograph: Dr James Rose, Ayr)

Figure 7 (c):
Monument to Jean Armour, wife
of Robert Burns, in Dumfries
(Photograph: Helen Braidwood, Dumfries)

Figure 7 (d):
Burns Cottage

Figure 7 (e):
Front: Robert Burns the poet
(Courtesy Clydesdale Bank)

Figure 7 (f): Royal Mint
Commemorative Stamp
(Courtesy Dr Ian Evans, Helensburgh, Argyll)

8. Sir WILLIAM BURRELL and The Burrell Collection (1861 – 1958)

KEY POINTS:

- Born in Glasgow.
- A wealthy shipping owner.

The Burrell Collection:

- The Burrell Collection is one of the finest personal collections of antiquities in the world. Sir William and Lady Burrell gave it to the city of Glasgow in 1944. This wonderful collection includes:
- Medieval and Renaissance art of Northern Europe, tapestries, stained glass and sculpture.
- Chinese art-porcelain, bronzes and furniture.
- European art, including works by Rembrandt, Chardin, Degas, Cezanne and Rodin.
- Islamic art.
- The art and artefacts of ancient civilizations.
- See figures: 8 (a) & (b)

Figure 8 (a): The Burrell Collection,
Pollock Country Park, Glasgow

Figure 8 (b): The Charity of a Beggar at Ornans
(Gustav Courbet, 1868, oil):
*(The Burrell Collection, Glasgow,
reproduced courtesy of Glasgow Museums)*

9.   ROBERT the BRUCE (1274 – 1329)

KEY POINTS:

- Born in Turnberry Castle in Ayrshire.
- Robert the Bruce was King of Scots (1309-1329).
- Led Scotland in the War of Scottish Independence and defeated the English at the Battle of Bannockburn in 1314.
- In 1320, submitted the Declaration of Arbroath to Pope John XXII, declaring Bruce as rightful monarch and asserting Scotland's status as an Independent Kingdom.
- Clydesdale Bank introduced a £20 banknote featuring Robert the Bruce in its Famous Scots Series.
- Died aged 54.
- See figures:9 (a) & (b)

Figure 9 (b):
Front: Robert the Bruce, a Scottish Warrior and King
(Courtesy Clydesdale Bank)

Figure 9 (a):
The Bruce Monument at Bannockburn
(Photograph: John Broadfoot, Stirling)

10. Sir HENRY CAMPBELL-BANNERMAN (1836 – 1908)

KEY POINTS:

Figure 10: Henry Campbell-Bannerman

- Born in Glasgow
- Created the modern Liberal Party.
- Initiated a system of social reform e.g. welfare state system, introduction of old age pensions, free meals and medical inspections for school children, job centres for the unemployed, greater rights for workers and trade unions.
- Prime Minister of Britain.
  He was the first man to be given the official title of "Prime Minister".
  (Liberal from 1905 to 1908).
- See figure 10

11. TONY BLAIR (1953 – present)

KEY POINTS:

Figure 11: Tony Blair

- Born in Edinburgh in 1953 and spent part of his childhood in Glasgow.
- Studied at Fettes School, Edinburgh.
- Elected Labour Leader in 1994.
- Within a short period transformed the Labour Party.
- Brought to an end eighteen years of Conservative government.
- Took Labour to a historic three terms of office.
- Youngest British Prime Minister at the age of 43 years. Longest serving Labour Prime Minister in history (from 1997 to 2007).
- Controversially supported the USA to invade Iraq. Oversaw the Northern Irish peace process, public sector reform and the response to 9/11 and 7/7 terrorist attacks. The Chilcot Report on Iraq War offers a devastating critique of Tony Blair.
- Master Statesman.
- He is the only living British prime minister to have appeared in an episode of The Simpsons. This and other instances of his instinct for self-promotion have earned him as much adverse criticism as praise.
- Blair is a lifelong fan of mainstream rock music. As a student, he was involved in promoting rock groups on the university circuit.
- See figure 11

12. GORDON BROWN (1951 – present)

KEY POINTS:

Figure 12: Gordon Brown

- Born in Glasgow and educated in Kirkcaldy, Fife.
- He was Rector of Edinburgh University while still a student.
- Became the 7th Scottish-born Prime Minister of United Kingdom (from 2007 to 2010).
- Before becoming Prime Minister he was Chancellor of the Exchequer for ten years, the longest continuously serving chancellor since the 1820's.
- His premiership was overshadowed by a banking crisis that led to a global economic recession and to mounting government debt, and unending conflict in Afghanistan.
- One of a very few genuine intellectuals in British political life – he holds a doctorate and was for some years a university lecturer – Brown's gifts are not those of a media savvy 21st century politician.
- Though a Labour politician, he – like his friend and rival Tony Blair – privately admired the Conservative Prime Minister Margaret Thatcher's 'free market' philosophy.
- Brown lost the only general election he ever fought as leader.
- See figure 12

13. ANDREW CARNEGIE (1835 – 1919)

KEY POINTS:

- Carnegie was born in Dunfermline, Scotland, in 1835.
- At the age of thirteen, after no more than a year or two of formal schooling, he set sail with his mother, father, and younger brother to America.
- After emigrating to America with his family, he rose from his job as a bobbin boy in a Pittsburgh cotton factory to become a telegraph messenger, Pennsylvania Railroad employee, bridge builder, iron and steel maker, and *eventually the richest man in the world*.
- Set up The Carnegie Steel Company.
- *Dedicated himself to a life of philanthropy.*
- Andrew Carnegie Paid Back His Debt To Mankind.
- See figures: 13 (a) & (b)

Figure 13 (a): A plaque in memory of Andrew Carnegie in Dunfermline

Figure 13 (b): A statue in memory of Andrew Carnegie in Dunfermline

14. THOMAS CARLYLE (1795 – 1881)

KEY POINTS:

- Born in Ecclefechan, Dumfriesshire.
- A figure of enormous importance in his time.
- A leading intellectual and moral force. A great Victorian scholar. A brilliant historian and original thinker.
- An idealist.
- Had Calvinist upbringing. He believed in God but could not accept the membership of any church.
- Believed in strong leadership, and that "Might is Right".
- Carlyle's works fell out of favour in the 20th century because of what was perceived as their implicit and explicit Fascist ideologies.
- Died in 1881 and buried in churchyard in Ecclefechan.
- See figure 14

Figure 14: Monument to Thomas Carlyle in Kelvingrove Park, Glasgow

14. Sir SEAN CONNERY (1930 – present)

KEY POINTS:

- Born and brought up in Edinburgh. Grew up in a tenement in Fountainbridge. It is the smoking industrial end of Edinburgh near the McCowan's toffee factory.
- He left school at thirteen and did not have any further formal education.
- Worked as a milkman, a lorry driver and enlisted in the Royal Navy.
- Reached international fame as an actor. Secret Agent 007 in six of Ian Fleming's James Bond movies. He starred in John Huston's memorable adaptation of Rudyard Kipling's adventure *The Man Who Would be King* and Brian De Palma's *The Untouchables*, for which he won an Oscar.
- Connery is to this day both respected and feared by the Hollywood film industry because of his very robust approach to business negotiations.
- Although he is undoubtedly an international superstar, Sir Sean Connery still knows the City of Edinburgh almost street by street from delivering the morning milk as a schoolboy. His round included Fettes College where Ian Fleming sent his fictional James Bond after he was expelled from Eton.
- *Sir Sean Connery stated that when he took a taxi during a recent Edinburgh Film Festival, the cabbie was amazed that he could put a name to every street they passed. "How come?" the cabbie asked. "As a boy I used to deliver milk round here", Connery said. "So what do you do now?"... That was rather harder to answer.*
- See figures: 15 (a) & (b)

Figure 15 (a): Sir Sean Connery

Figure 15 (b): Milk Cart
(Courtesy of Graham's The Family Dairy Group Limited, Scotland)

16. BILLY CONNOLLY (1942 – present)

KEY POINTS:

- Billy Connolly was born on 24th November, 1942 in Anderston, Glasgow. In his early teens the family moved to Drumchapel.
- Billy qualified as a welder. He graduated with a first class degree in comedy banter while training in the Clydeside shipyards.
- In the mid 70's Connolly's star status was establshed. He is the most successful British stand-up comedian of today. It is clear that his humour has got him through life.
- His live shows in the 1970s often contained highly controversial material. His monologue on the Crucifixion offended many, and in his willingness to shock his audiences he began a tradition of Scottish confrontational comedy continued today in the work of Frankie Boyle and others.
- He was immortalised in a full colour comic strip, titled 'The Big Yin', in the late 1970s Sunday edition of *The Daily Record*.
- Connolly reached number one in the pop charts in 1975 with a parody version of the country and western song D.I.V.O.R.C.E. He is himself a songwriter, and was, with the late Gerry Rafferty, part of a folk music act called The Humblebums.
- See figure 16

Figure 16: Billy Connolly

17. Dr ARCHIBALD JOSEPH CRONIN (1896 – 1981)

KEY POINTS:

Figure 17: A.J. Cronin
(Courtesy Dumbarton Library, Dumbarton)

- Born in Cardross, Dunbartonshire on 19th July, 1896.
- Graduated MBChB with honours at Glasgow University in 1919.
- He practised medicine in Scotland, Wales and London in Harley Street.
- His first great book *Hatter's Castle* was published in 1931 and led to his rapid rise to the front rank among novelists. Following this success, his second novel *The Citadel* portrayed a doctor struggling against cynicism, describing shady London private medical practice. However, its success encouraged Cronin to abandon medicine for the career of an author.
- Several of his best-selling novels were made into feature films.
- In 1962 the BBC produced the television series *Dr Finlay's Casebook* based on Cronin's experiences as a young doctor in Scotland. Homely tales of Scottish general practice (from 1962– 1971).
- Cronin moved to Switzerland and died there in 1981, aged 84.
- See figure 17

18. WILLIAM CULLEN (1710 – 1790)

KEY POINTS:

Figure 18: William Cullen
(Courtesy Royal College of Physicians of Edinburgh)

- Born Hamilton, Lanarkshire, Scotland.
- A Scottish physician, chemist and agriculturalist. One of the most important professors at the Edinburgh Medical School. A polymath.
- Author of popular medical textbook *First Lines of the Practice of Physics*.
- Scottish Enlightenment figure.
- He was President of the Royal College of Physicians and Surgeons of Glasgow, President of the Royal College of Physicians of Edinburgh and First Physician to the King in Scotland (1773-1790).
- Died in Edinburgh, 5th February 1790.
- See figure 18

19. Sir JAMES DEWAR (1842 – 1923)

KEY POINTS:

- Born in Fife.
- Studied chemistry at Edinburgh University.
- Best known for his work on the liquefaction of gases and low temperature technology.
- Invented the Vacuum Flask but did not patent his invention.
- Dewar was a scientist not a businessman.
- Later in 1904 two German glassblowers began to produce the flask commercially and renamed it Thermos after the Greek word thermos, meaning heat.
- He is also credited with inventing cordite.
- See figure 19

Figure 19: The Vacuum Flask or Thermos Flask

20. DONALD DEWAR (1937 – 2000)

KEY POINTS:

- Dewar was born in Glasgow.
- Obtained MA in History and LLB degrees from Glasgow University.
- President of the Glasgow University Union.
- Worked as a solicitor in Glasgow.
- Became an MP in 1966 (Aberdeen South) but lost his seat in 1970. Re-elected to Westminster at a by-election in 1978 in Glasgow, Garscadden. Campaigned for a Scottish parliament in the failed referendum in 1979 but eventually led the successful devolution campaign in 1997.
- Dewar was a bibliophile and an avid collector of documents important in Scottish life, politics and literature.
- Started the devolution process and worked tirelessly on creating the Scotland Act. This was ratified and gave Scotland its first Scottish Parliament in 1999.
- Nominated First Minister of Scotland and served 17th May, 1999 to 11th October, 2000.
- Died on 11th October, 2000, aged 63.
- See figure 20

Figure 20 : In 2002, a nine-foot (2.7m) bronze statue of Dewar was erected outside Glasgow's Royal Concert Hall

21. Sir ARTHUR CONAN DOYLE (1859 – 1930)

KEY POINTS:

- Born in Edinburgh.
- Studied medicine at Edinburgh University and practised medicine in Portsmouth.
- Gave up the practice of medicine and became a very famous novelist.
- Conan Doyle, unlike his creation Holmes, was a believer in spiritualism for much of his life.
- Creator of the world's most famous private detective – Sherlock Holmes, whose stories he wrote.
- A first edition, with dust jacket, of his novella *The Hound of the Baskervilles* is one of the most sought after books of the 20th century.
- The skills of Mr Sherlock Holmes were based on the following attributes and thus able to solve murder mysteries (The Science of Deduction):
  - Knowledge of chemistry - profound.
  - Knowledge of human anatomy - precise.

Figure 21 : Sherlock Holmes the detective
(Picardy Place, Edinburgh - the birthplace of Conan Doyle)

  - Knowledge of sensational literature - immense. Mr Holmes appears to know every detail of every horror perpetuated in the century.
  - Knowledge of geology - practical. Could tell at a glance one soil from another.
  - Knowledge of botany - good. Well up in belladonna, opium and poisons generally.
- Sir Arthur Conan Doyle died in 1930.
- See figure 21

22. IAN DONALD (1910 – 1987)

- Born in Cornwall but grew up in Scotland.
- Graduated in medicine in 1937. Educated first in Edinburgh then in South Africa.
- Became Professor of Midwifery at Glasgow University.
- Produced the first diagnostic, 2-dimensional Obstetric Ultrasound Scanner.
- In 1958 Donald published the first ultrasound image of a moving foetus. Soon ultrasound machines emerged and the technique was of revolutionary importance in medicine.
- Donald opposed the 1967 Abortion Act.
- Donald lived to see ultrasound in worldwide routine use.
- See figure 22

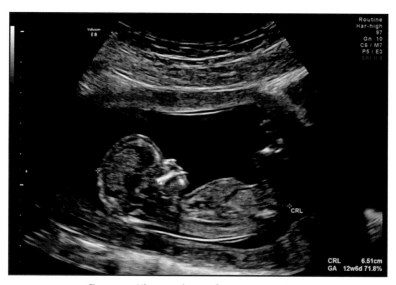

Figure 22 : Ultrasound scan of a pregnant mother
(Courtesy Dr Iain McGlinchey, Helensburgh, Argyll)

23. JOHN BOYD DUNLOP (1840 – 1921)

KEY POINTS:

Figure 23 : Dunlop pneumatic tyre

- Born at Dreghorn, Ayrshire, Scotland.
- Practised as a veterinary surgeon.
- Re-invented the pneumatic tyre in 1887 and patented it in 1888. Unknown to him, Dunlop discovered that almost 40 years earlier another Scot, Robert William Thomson, from Stonehaven, had invented the pneumatic tyre, called it the "aerial wheel", and patented it.
- Formed the Dunlop Pneumatic Tyre Company and became one of the largest tyre manufacturers in the world.
- Dunlop died aged 81.
- See figure 23

24. HENRY FAULDS (1843 – 1930)

KEY POINTS:

Figure 24 : Fingerprint, with enlargement showing pores, like a railway map with stations

- Faulds, of Scottish descent, was born on 1st June, 1843, in Ayrshire.
- Studied medicine at Anderson's College, Glasgow and passed his final examination as a Licentiate of the Royal Faculty of Physicians and Surgeons in Glasgow.
- His strong religious convictions inclined him towards foreign missionary work and he worked as a missionary in India and Japan.
- Faulds was the pioneer of our modern police fingerprinting methods by which criminals are identified from finger impressions left at crime scenes. A dactylography means an imprint of fingers or toes, or of a single finger or toe.
- Our finger patterns are unique in every individual, irrespective of race and sex. He said these patterns were "forever unchangeable". Thus finger impressions would be of advantage in the detection of crimes such as murder or theft. *No one prior to Faulds had recognised their forensic importance. He led a complete revolution in criminal detective methods.*
- According to *The Glasgow Herald* of 20th March, 1930, in its short obituary notice, Faulds was "the pioneer of the path in opening up the system of fingerprints in crime detection".
- See figure 24

25. Sir ALEXANDER FLEMING (1881 – 1955)

KEY POINTS:

- Born in Darvel, East Ayrshire, in 1888.
- Studied medicine at St Mary's Hospital Medical School, London.
- Became a brilliant bacteriologist, biologist and pharmacologist.
- Discovered the enzyme lysozyme in 1922.
- In September 1928, he noticed a strange blue-green mould had grown on the culture in a Petri dish. Nearly threw the dish into the bin, but realised something was different and that the mould had killed off all the bacteria in the dish it had come into contact with.
- He named the mould penicillin from the Latin *Penicillium chrysogeneum (formerly P. notatum)*.
- He continued to work on penicillin but was unable to discover how to produce enough of the antibiotic. He abandoned the penicillin project and moved on to other research.
- A team of Oxford University scientists led by Howard Florey and Ernst Boris Chain returned to Fleming's work. Alexander Fleming was never invited to work with Florey and Chain, but it was never forgotten that Fleming was the man who discovered penicillin in the first place. In 1941 they made the crucial breakthrough and enabled this natural antibiotic to be synthesized and produced in a form effective in the treatment of infections.
- In 1945 the Nobel Prize for Medicine was awarded to all three men, Florey, Chain and Fleming. Fleming in his Nobel Prize acceptance speech warned that inappropriate use of antibiotics would give rise to resistance. Fleming's prediction has come to pass and antibiotic resistance is now threatening modern medicine.

Figure 25 (a): Front, Sir Alexander Fleming, the Scottish biologist and pharmacologist
(Courtesy Clydesdale Bank)

- The first patient to be treated by the wonder drug penicillin was an Oxford policeman dying of septicaemia.
- Fleming said, *"One sometimes finds what one is not looking for."*- Serendipitous discovery.
- Clydesdale Bank launched a £5 banknote featuring Sir Alexander Fleming in the World Heritage Series of banknotes.
- See figures: 25 (a) & (b)

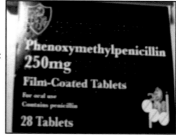

Figure 25 (b): Penicillin tablets

26. WILLIAM EWART GLADSTONE (1809 – 1898)

KEY POINTS:

- He was born in Liverpool to a wealthy Scottish merchant. His father was a corn dealer in Edinburgh and Leith, the family having moved to the capital from the village of Biggar in the Scottish Borders. Later the family moved from Leith to Liverpool.
- Educated at Eton and the University of Oxford.
- He was a famous Liberal Prime Minister on four occasions. (From 1892 to 1894, 1886 to 1886, 1880 to 1885 and 1868 to 1874).
- He was one of the world's greatest orators in the classical style.
- He always wore a glove or a finger-stall to hide a forefinger mutilated in a shooting accident.
- See figures: 26 (a) & (b)

Figure 26 (a): Monument to William Ewart Gladstone, George Square, Glasgow

Figure 26 (b):
Gladstone bag: J.G. Beard is credited with inventing the Gladstone bag and naming it in honour of the four-time 19th century British Prime Minister, William Ewart Gladstone. Beard, a leather trader, was an admirer of Gladstone and knew of his love of travel, so Beard named the bag after him. Gladstone bags are also known as doctors' bags because of their popularity within medical profession.

27. Sir CHRIS HOY (1976 – present)

KEY POINTS:

- Born in Edinburgh.
- The world's greatest cyclist.
- Britain's most successful Olympian of all time.
- He won a total of six Olympic golds and one silver, making him Britain's most successful Olympic athlete and the most decorated cyclist of all time.
- It is appropriate that Scotland's greatest Olympian happens to be a cyclist, as the bicycle was invented in Dumfries and Galloway.
- He was knighted in 2009. Chris Hoy said with modesty, *"To become a knight from riding your bike? It's mad! It feels a bit strange and I still can't take it in"*.
- See figures 27: (a) & (b)

Figure 27 (a): Sir Chris Hoy

Figure 27 (b): Gold painted post-box in Hanover Street, Edinburgh. (In honour of Sir Chris Hoy).

28. DAVID HUME (1711 – 1776)

KEY POINTS:

- Hume was born in Edinburgh.
- 18th century Scottish Philosopher. David Hume is one of the world's great philosophers. At the age of 25, he wrote one of the greatest masterpieces of thought ever written in the English language. He was an economist and an influential enlightenment philosopher.
- Published his best known work *A Treatise of Human Nature*.
- Ironically, Hume was considered exceptionally dim as a child, due to his habit of asking odd questions like - Why doesn't water run uphill?
- He proposed that Christianity and religion in general was a matter of faith and not a matter of fact. Everything had to be proven and God was no exception, though he never called himself an atheist. Today he might be more correctly described as an agnostic.
- He rejected Christian orthodoxy and foretold crises of faith versus scientific knowledge. He promoted a radical philosophical empiricism.
- He died in Edinburgh in 1776 of intestinal cancer.
- See figure 28

Figure 28: Memorial to David Hume in High Street, Edinburgh.

29. HUNTER BROTHERS - John Hunter (1728 – 1793), William Hunter (1718 – 1783)

KEY POINTS:

- John Hunter and William Hunter were brothers born in Long Calderwood, East Kilbride, Lanarkshire. Became major figures in world medicine.
- William Hunter studied medicine at the University of Glasgow. His life's work was to improve the quality and safety of childbirth.
- William Hunter enjoyed success as an anatomy teacher, surgeon and man-midwife (eventually becoming physician to Queen Charlotte).The collection that brought him lasting fame – the Hunterian Museum and Art Gallery, University of Glasgow.
- John Hunter became one of the leading surgeons of his time. He is the acknowledged founder of modern surgery. In London John Hunter became the most celebrated surgeon of his generation. He excelled as a surgeon, anatomist, naturalist and collector.
- See figures: 29 (a) & (b)

Figure 29 (a): John Hunter
(Courtesy Royal College of Physicians of Edinburgh)

Figure 29 (b): William Hunter
(Courtesy Royal College of Physicians of Edinburgh)

30. KEIR HARDIE (1856 – 1915)

KEY POINTS:

- Born in Bellshill, North Lanarkshire in a one-roomed house.
- He worked down the mines as a "trapper" – opening and closing a door for a ten hour shift in order to maintain the air supply for miners.
- Had no formal schooling.
- Led the radical movement which resulted in the founding of the Scottish Labour Party in 1888 and the Independent Labour Party (ILP) in 1893. The ILP was affiliated to the Labour Representative Committee (LRC), which became the Labour Party in 1906.
- First leader of the Labour Party.
- In 1900 became Labour's first ever Member of Parliament for Merthyr, Wales.
- A dedicated socialist, Christian and pacifist.
- Hardie was also a lay preacher and temperance campaigner who supported votes for

Figure 30: Keir Hardie

women, home rule for India and an end to segregation in South Africa.
- There are now 40 streets throughout Britain named after him.
- See figure 30

31. ELSIE MAUD INGLIS (1864 – 1917)

KEY POINTS:

- Scottish by parentage and residence but not by place of birth.
- Elsie Inglis, the sixth of eight children, was born at Naini Tal in the foothills of the Himalayas.
- Trained as a doctor in Edinburgh and Glasgow.
- In1894, opened a maternity hospital for the poor women of Edinburgh, staffed entirely by women.
- Played an important part in the founding of the Scottish Federation of Women's Suffrage Societies.
- During the First World War she set up the Scottish Women's Hospitals, staffed solely by women.
- She advanced the cause of female equality.
- Clydesdale Bank issued a £50 banknote featuring Elsie Maud Inglis, in the World Heritage Series.
- See figures: 31 (a) & (b)

Figure 31 (a): Front: This note bears a portrait of Elsie Maud Inglis, who in 1894 jointly established in Edinburgh a maternity hospital for poor women, staffed entirely by women.
(Courtesy Clydesdale Bank)

Figure 31 (b): Elsie Maud Inglis

32. WILLIAM JARDINE (1784 – 1843) and JAMES MATHESON (1796 – 1878) and THOMAS BLAKE GLOVER (1838 – 1911)

KEY POINTS:

- The firm of Jardine Matheson and Co was begun in Canton, China on 1stJuly 1832 by University of Edinburgh Medical School graduate William Jardine and University of Edinburgh graduate James Matheson. Jardine was born on a small farm near Lochmaben, Dumfriesshire. Thomas Blake Glover was born in Fraserburgh and died in Tokyo. Mr Glover was a businessman who worked initially for Jardine Matheson in China and Japan. He later developed his own trading interests in Japan and is credited with considerable influence on the country's internal politics – opening it up to foreign trade and industrialisation. He is better known in Japan than in his native country.
- *Exported tea from China and in return supplied the Chinese with smuggled opium, which was imported from British India.*
- *Chairman Mao eradicated the opium trade in China with a public health strategy.*
- After the 1949 foundation of the People's Republic of China, trading conditions for foreign companies under the new communist regime became increasingly difficult.
- Jardine Matheson Holdings remains the largest Asian-based multinational commercial company in Hong Kong.
- While the leadership of Jardines is Scottish, the firm is international in its dealings.
- Mail sent to Jardines requires no address –the name alone is enough to ensure its delivery.
- See figure 32

Figure 32:
1846 view of Jardine's
original building from
Causeway Bay in Hong Kong

33. JOHN KNOX (1512 – 1572)

KEY POINTS:

- Born in Haddington (East Lothian).
- Historic religious figure-theologian.
- Public face of the Reformation in Scotland. He is credited with the authorship of *The First Book of Discipline*, a blueprint for a 'new' Scotland.
- Transformed Scotland from Catholicism to Protestantism and came into conflict with Mary Queen of Scots.
- Established the Church of Scotland.
- Founding father of Presbyterianism.
- Calvinism established in Scotland under the influence of Knox.
- A democrat and believer in both education and social welfare for all. He envisaged a school in every parish in the land.
- Buried in Edinburgh under the St Giles Cathedral car park.
- See figures: 33 (a) & (b)

Figure 33 (a):
Monument to John Knox at the Necropolis of Glagow

Figure 33 (b):
John Knox dispensing the Sacrament at Calder House, West Lothian

34. THOMAS LIPTON (1850 – 1931)

KEY POINTS:

- Born in the Gorbals in Glasgow.
- Established his first grocer's shop in Glasgow in 1871. By 1890, he had more than 150 stores throughout Britain.
- Lipton bought five tea plantations in Ceylon (now Sri Lanka) and supplied tea direct to his own stores. *Advertised his tea as "coming straight from the plantation to the pot".*
- Lipton Yellow Label is sold all over the world and remains one of the most popular brands.
- See figure 34

Figure 34: Lipton Yellow Label tea

35. JAMES LIND (1716 – 1794)

KEY POINTS:

- He was born in Edinburgh, the son of an Edinburgh merchant.
- Studied medicine, graduated MD from Edinburgh University in 1748 and served in the Royal navy as a ship's surgeon.
- For mariners scurvy was a killer. Lind (in 1747) organised the world's first controlled clinical trial in medicine. Lind reported his findings in *A Treatise of the Scurvy* and recommended that citrus fruit should become a regular part of the diet at sea. This was at a time when scurvy was a major cause of morbidity and mortality in the Royal Navy, the force on which Britain's political and military supremacy depended. *It is reported that a million British seamen died of scurvy in the 18th Century. Thereafter, British sailors were called "Limeys".*
- It was in 1933 that the ascorbic acid was isolated in citrus fruit and given the name vitamin C.
- See figures 35: (a), (b) & (c)

Figure 35 (a): James Lind
(Reproduced Courtesy of Royal College of Physicians of Edinburgh)

Figure 35 (b): Oranges and Limes

Figure 35 (c): Ascorbic acid (vitamin C) tablets

36. ERIC LIDDELL (1902 – 1945)

- Eric Henry Liddell was born in Tientsin (Tianjin) in China to Scottish missionary parents. He had a shy, self-effacing personality. He showed gentleness, sportsmanship and genuine concern for others.
- Eric Liddell took 47.6 seconds to win the 400 metres race at the 1924 Paris Olympic Games. This famous victory has now become a timeless moment in modern sporting history. Liddell made progress from gifted childhood athlete to rising track star at the University of Edinburgh.
- In addition to the sporting side of Eric Liddell, he had a religious commitment leading to missionary work in China. He accomplished so much in sport and committed himself wholeheartedly to the work of Christian mission. The two were intertwined in his life.
- The inspiring film *Chariots of Fire* reminded the world of Eric Liddell, who ran for gold at the Paris Olympics in 1924.
- A key point of his Christian witness was his attitude to Sunday as the Lord's Day. He sacrificed his strong chance of winning the Olympic Games blue ribbon 100 metres sprint event because the competition schedule clashed with his Christian beliefs.
- His Christian beliefs aside, Liddell's austere individualism and indifference to the trappings of wealth and fame influenced the creation of two major characters in the children's comics of the 1960s and 1970s: 'Wilson' and 'Tupper, the Tough of the Track'.
- He was taken prisoner by the Japanese. The Japanese had made a deal with the British, with Churchill's approval, for the exchange of a few selected prisoners. Liddell was chosen for exchange but gave up his chance of repatriation to a woman in the camp who was pregnant. Liddell is adored in China after caring for fellow prisoners of the Japanese in the Second World War. **Eric Liddell is a National Hero in China**.
- Today, there stands a monument to him on the site of the former Weihsien Internment Camp, and his home has been protected as a historical site in China.
- *Liddell's sportsmanship and Christian integrity must stand as a constant inspiration to the youth of today to live by Christian principles in every area of life.*
- He died in China from a brain tumour in 1945.
- See figures: 36 (a), (b), (c) & (d)

Figure 36 (a): British Empire versus United States of America (relay race) meet held at Stamford Bridge on Saturday 19th July, 1924.
(Courtesy Wikipedia, the Free Encyclopedia)

Figure 36 (b): Olympic Gold Medal won by Eric Liddell

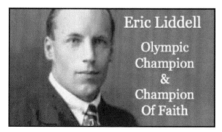

Figure 36 (c): Eric Liddell Olympic Champion and Champion of Faith

Figure 36 (d): Monument to Eric Liddell in the grounds of the former Weihsien Internment Camp

37.   Lord LISTER (1827 – 1912)

KEY POINTS:

Figure 37 (a): Monument to Lord Joseph Lister in Kelvingrove Park, Glasgow

- Born into a Quaker family in West Ham, England.
- Lister was educated in England and graduated from London University.
- Although not a Scot he worked as Regius Professor of Surgery at Glasgow University and Glasgow Royal Infirmary and was Professor of Clinical Surgery at Edinburgh University.
- He introduced antiseptic techniques in the operating theatre. While working in Scotland, he produced his ideas on reducing the incidence of infection following surgery. Lister began to apply a dressing soaked in a solution of carbolic acid in twenty parts of water on the wounds to prevent germs from gaining access to the damaged tissues.
- His important work on the cause and prevention of septic infection of wounds was done at Glasgow Royal Infirmary.
- He was made a baronet, Sir Joseph Lister, and in 1897 became Lord Lister.
- He died in 1912.
- See figures: 37 (a), (b) & (c)

Figure 37 (b): Royal Mail commemorative stamp: Lister's Carbolic Spray
(Courtesy Dr Ian Evans, Helensburgh, Argyll)

Figure 37 (c): Royal Mail commemorative stamp: Lister's and Chemical Symbols
(Courtesy Dr Ian Evans, Helensburgh, Argyll)

38. DAVID LIVINGSTONE (1813 – 1873)

KEY POINTS:

- Born in Blantyre in South Lanarkshire.
- Worked in the local cotton mill as a piecer, his job being to join together the broken threads.
- Studied medicine at Anderson's University, Glasgow. At the same time he attended Greek and theology classes at Glasgow University, and became an ordained minister.
- He was the first white man to explore the wildest part of central Africa. A journey down the Zambezi River brought him to one of the greatest wonders of the world. Livingstone named the great waterfall the Victoria Falls after the then reigning Queen.
- Acclaimed by the Protestant church as one of the greatest missionaries, and by the Royal Geographical Society as one of its greatest explorers. However, his mission to save the people of Central Africa by bringing them Christianity failed.
- It was due to Livingstone's work and writings that the movement was set up which abolished the slave trade in Africa.
- Ironically, Livingstone's life and legend informed the writing of Joseph Conrad's most famous novel, the deeply pessimistic *Heart of Darkness*.
- No one in the UK had had any news of Livingstone for four and a half years. In order to find out what had happened to him, a young man, Stanley, was sent to Africa by an American newspaper. Stanley found Livingstone. This is how he described the meeting: *"I took off my hat and said 'Dr Livingstone I presume?' 'Yes,' he said with a kind smile and we shook hands."* It is one of the most famous meetings in history.
- Livingstone had discovered Victoria Falls, Lake Ngami, Lake Malawi, and Lake Bangweulu. He had explored the course of several rivers and mapped parts of Central Africa for the first time.
- His body is buried in Westminster Abbey, London.
- See figures: 38 (a), (b), (c) & (d)

Figure 38 (a): Royal Mail commemorative stamp - David Livingstone
(Courtesy Dr Ian Evans, Helensburgh, Argyll)

Figure 38 (b): Portrait of David Livingstone
(Reproduced Courtesy of
Royal College of Physicians and Surgeons of Glasgow)

Figure 38 (c): Monument to David
Livingstone in Cathedral Square, Glasgow

Figure 38 (d): A bronze statue at The David Livingstone Centre, Blantyre.
"He shook me as a terrier does a rat" David Livingstone

39. KILPATRICK MACMILLAN (1812 – 1878)

Figure 39: World's oldest bicycle.
In Glasgow Transport Museum.
(Reproduced Courtesy of Glasgow Museums)

- He was born in Keir, Dumfries and Galloway, the son of a blacksmith.
- Macmillan developed the first rear-wheel powered bicycle, driven by means of pedals connected to levers attached to the rear wheel.
- This world-changing invention was never actually patented by its inventor and was widely copied.
- Macmillan rode from Dumfries to Glasgow, no fewer than 70 miles, to reach his destination. It took him two days. He apparently knocked over a small girl who ran across his path in the Gorbals in Glasgow. He was fined five shillings for "furious driving" and general negligence. I gather the judge was so impressed by the bike that he paid the fine himself. His bike is on display in the Glasgow Transport Museum.
- See figure 39

40. CHARLES MACINTOSH (1766 – 1843)

Figure 40: Waterproof
"The Macintosh coat"
(Reproduced Courtesy of Lara Wilkinson, Helensburgh, Arygll)

- Born in Glasgow.
- Worked as a chemist in Glasgow.
- He opened the first alum factory in Scotland and produced dyestuffs.
- Used naphtha dissolved India rubber between two layers of cloth, which penetrated the pores of the cloth. The naphtha evaporated, leaving the cloth waterproof. This was the breakthrough; *waterproof cloth had been invented.*
- Began manufacturing waterproof coats-rain coats named, **mac** or **mack** or **The Macintosh**. Subsequently used in an expedition to the Arctic in 1824.
- For this and other chemical discoveries he was elected a Fellow of the Royal Society in 1823.
- See figure 40

41. WILLIAM MURDOCH (1754 – 1839)

KEY POINTS:

Figure 41: Gas lighting outside Free Church, Dumbarton

- Born in Auchinleck in Ayrshire, the son of a mill designer.
- Invented gas lighting using gas made from coal. He lit his own house with gas lamps as early as 1792.
- Thereafter, gas lamps appeared on the streets of cities, eventually being replaced by electric lights.
- He also produced the first model of a steam carriage, a small tricycle with a steam engine driving the wheels through a piston.
- See figure 41

42. JAMES CLERK MAXWELL (1831 – 1879)

KEY POINTS:

Figure 42: James Clerk Maxwell

- Born in Edinburgh.
- Professor of Natural Philosophy at Marischal College, Aberdeen; Professor of Natural Philosophy, King's College, London; First Professor of Experimental Physics at Cambridge.
- A Scottish Physicist. Wrote *A Treatise on Electricity and Magnetism*, published in 1873.
- Maxwell's discovery of the laws of electromagnetism has been described as the most significant event of the 19th century.
- Discovered that by mixing the primary colours of red, green and blue one could produce the colour white.
- Produced the world's first colour photograph in 1861.
- Maxwell discovered that people who were colour-blind and could not distinguish between green and blue lacked red-sensitive receptors.
- He determined that the rings of Saturn were composed of numerous small particles, all independently orbiting the planet. At the time it was generally thought the rings were solid. The Maxwell Ringlet and Maxwell Gap were named in his honour.
- He was a devout Christian all his life.
- He died in 1879 of cancer of the colon at 48 years of age.
- See figure 42

43. ANDY MURRAY (1987 – present)

KEY POINTS:

- Born in Dunblane, near Stirling.
- Britain's most successful tennis player.
- Andy became the first British player to win a Wimbledon singles title since 1977 and the first British man to win the Men's Singles Championship since Fred Perry more than seven decades previously.
- Won Davis Cup Final 2015. Led Great Britain to first title in 79 years.
- Wimbledon singles champion 2016, second time in 80 years.
- Rio de Janeiro 2016: Andy Murray becomes first male player to win two Olympic tennis golds after beating Juan Martin del Porto. Andy said *"Any athlete will give his best to be here and having this (Olympic medal) around my neck is a dream for any sportsman. To have the chance to have two is much more than a dream."*
- Received BBC's Sports Personality of the Year Award in 2015
- He opened a five star hotel "CROMLIX" close to his home town of Dunblane. It has a tennis court in the Wimbledon colours. Cromlix is a good base for a tour of central Scotland and the Highlands, or for golfers wanting to play at nearby Gleneagles.
- He said *"To succeed you need a mind-set to work hard and a positive attitude".*
- Murray recently became number one in the worldwide tennis rankings.
- See figures: 43 (a), (b), (c) & (d)

Figure 43 (a): Andy Murray, tennis champion

Figure 43 (b): Andy Murray's, Cromlix Hotel, Dunblane

Figure 43 (c): Tennis court in the Wimbledon colours at Cromlix Hotel, Dunblane

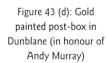

Figure 43 (d): Gold painted post-box in Dunblane (in honour of Andy Murray)

44. JOHN LOUDON MCADAM (1756 – 1836)

KEY POINTS:

- Born in Ayr in 1756.
- Revolutionised road construction around the world: ROADMAKER.
- McAdam's improvements became known as "macadamisation". Known as tarmacadam or tarmac for short, it allowed the creation of a network of properly built roads. Soon every road in this country and many others were transformed.
- He did not, however, invent tarmacadam. That was the brainwave of a county surveyor in Nottingham in 1901.If a barrel of tar is spilt on the road it will produce a hard, smooth and dust-free surface.
- He died at the age of 80.
- See figures 44 (a) and (b)

Figure 44 (a): Macadamised road near Helensburgh, Argyll

Figure 44 (b): Plaque erected in memory of John Loudon McAdam by The Institution of Civil Engineers *(Photograph: Dr James Rose, Ayr)*

Over the centuries, great Scots have earned their place in history for numerous things.

45. CHARLES RENNIE MACKINTOSH (1868 – 1928)

KEY POINTS:

- Born in Glasgow.
- Trained as an architect in Glasgow and studied drawing at the Glasgow School of Art.
- Not only an architect, but a painter and innovator of a unique furniture style. In fact he is the Complete Artist, and it was his contribution to the new art that identifies him as a particular kind of genius.
- His legacy in our own time is at least as much commercial as artistic: the Mackintosh 'brand' can be found on everything from greetings cards to tee shirts.
- Designed the following buildings for which he is most famous:
  a. The Hill House in Helensburgh.
  b. The Glasgow School of Art in Renfrew Street, Garnethill, Glasgow.
  c. The Willow Tearooms in Glasgow.
  d. Queen's Cross Church, Glasgow.
  e. The Lighthouse, Charles Rennie Mackintosh's Glasgow Herald building.
  f. The House for An Art lover in Bellahouston Park, Glasgow.
  g. Scotland Street School in Glasgow.
  h. The Mackintosh House, Glasgow University.
- Clydesdale Bank launched a £100 banknote featuring Charles Rennie Mackintosh in the World Heritage Series.
- Developed cancer of the tongue and died in London, aged 60.
- See figures: 45 (a) & (b)

Figure 45 (a): The Hill House, Helensburgh, Argyll

Figure 45 (b): Front: The note features Charles Rennie Mackintosh, celebrated around the world as one of the most creative figures of the 20th century. *(Courtesy Clydesdale Bank)*

46. Sir WILLIAM MACEWEN (1848 – 1924)

KEY POINTS:

- Born on a farm near Rothesay on the Isle of Bute.
- Studied medicine at Glasgow University.
- Became Regius Professor of Clinical Surgery at Glasgow Royal Infirmary.
- Pioneer in both neurosurgery and bone graft techniques.
- In 1879 he performed the first viable bone graft.
- In 1895 he was the first to successfully remove a patient's tuberculous lung (pneumonectomy).
- He was instrumental in setting up Erskine Hospital for injured service men and women, and in particular those with limb injuries.
- See figure 46

Figure 46: Sir William MacEwen
(Reproduced courtesy of Royal College of Physicians and Surgeons Glasgow)

47. JOHN MUIR (1838 – 1914)

KEY POINTS:

- Born in Dunbar, East Lothian.
- Studied geology and botany.
- Naturalist and conservationist.
- He emigrated to America in 1849, settling in Wisconsin.
- He prompted President Theodore Roosevelt to create America's first National Park.
- Muir is referred to as the Father of America's National Parks. Muir's importance has long been acknowledged in the US with over 200 sites of scenic beauty named after him. Due to the movement he started, some 360 million acres of wilderness are now protected.

Figure 47: John Muir

- In Scotland, the John Muir Trust has reserves throughout the country, including areas in East Lothian, Knoydart, Skye and Sutherland.
- He is considered one of the key figures in the history of world ecology and environmentalism.
- See figure 47

48. JAMES RAMSAY MACDONALD (1866 – 1937)

KEY POINTS:

Figure 48: Ramsay MacDonald

- Born in Lossiemouth in Moray, in a two-roomed cottage.
- In 1911 he became the leader of the Labour Party and Britain's first working class Labour Prime Minister. (Labour, from 1929 to 1935, 1924 to 1924)
- He wrote the book *The Awakening of India* – one of the best books written about India.
- He opposed Britain's entry into the First World War.
- He said: "We hear war called murder. It is not: it is suicide."
- See figure 48

49. JOHN NAPIER (1550 – 1617)

KEY POINTS:

- Born in Merchiston Castle in Edinburgh, which is now part of the university named after him.
- An eminent mathematician.
- Theorised the concept of logarithms and the decimal point.
- Introduced logarithms to the world.
- He promoted the use of the decimal point.
- His idea of logarithm tables also led to the development of the slide rule, a calculating device used by scientists and engineers until 1970.
- He also invented war machines including the forerunners of the armoured tank and the submarine.
- See figures: 49 (a) & (b)

Figure 49 (a): Monument to John Napier
(Courtesy Wikipedia, the Free Encyclopaedia)

Figure 49 (b): Napier's Calculating Tables
(Courtesy Wikipedia, the Free Encyclopaedia)

50. WILLIAM RAMSAY (1852 – 1916)

KEY POINTS:

- Born in Glasgow.
- Studied chemistry at Glasgow University.
- Discovered, Krypton, Argon, Neon, Xenon and Helium. Argon was the first of the new elements Ramsay discovered and as he discovered more he gave them names that reflected their novelty- e.g. Neon, which is classical Greek for "new"; Krypton Xenon, which means "stranger" or alien.
- Neon had the greatest impact because it gives off a luminous red glow when electricity is conducted through it – used for neon signs for advertising.
- Helium has been popular for use in balloons.
- In 1904, he was recipient of a Nobel Prize for achievements in the field of chemistry.
- See figure 50

Figure 50: William Ramsay - working

Scottish physicians and surgeons have led the field in medical innovation.

51. J K ROWLING (1965 – Present)

KEY POINTS:

- Born in Gloucestershire in 1965, but has lived in Scotland for most of her adult life and wrote her Harry Potter novels while living in Edinburgh.
- Graduated from Exeter University in 1987, with a degree in modern languages.
- She wrote about Harry Potter in her first book, which was read by millions of children and adults all over the world.
- She is probably the most popular and successful writer of books for children.
- Her work, while hugely successful, is highly derivative. The Harry Potter books draw, for example, on sources as diverse as the work of JRR Tolkien and the boarding school stories of Enid Blyton.
- Harry Potter series:
  - *Harry Potter and the Philosopher's Stone* (First book, 1997)
  - *Harry Potter and the Chamber of Secrets*
  - *Harry Potter and the Prisoner of Azkaban*
  - *Harry Potter and the Goblet of Fire*
  - *Harry Potter and the Order of the Phoenix*
  - *Harry Potter and the Deathly Hallows*
  - *Harry Potter and the Half-Blood Prince*
  - Also published adult fiction: *The Casual Vacancy* (2012) and *The Cuckoo's Calling* (2013)
- *Harry Potter and the Philosopher's Stone* was made into a film and others soon followed.
- She was awarded an OBE for services to children's literature.
- See figure 51

Figure 51: Children reading Harry Potter books in Helensburgh Library, Helensburgh, Argyll

52. ALEX SALMOND (1954 – Present)

KEY POINTS:

Figure 52 (a): Alex Salmond

- He was born on Hogmanay 1954, in Linlithgow, West Lothian.
- Studied at St Andrews University.
- Became an SNP MP, aged 32.
- Major figure in Scottish politics. First Nationalist to lead the devolved Scottish Government as First Minister (2007-2014).
- The most capable and intriguing politician Scotland has produced in recent decades, he is not without his critics, who take pleasure in pointing out the apparent contradiction between his socialist rhetoric and his accommodating attitude towards big business.
- See figures: 52 (a), (b) & (c)

Figure 52 (b): Alex Salmond and Nicola Sturgeon at the National Conversation Launch

Figure 52 (c): Alex Salmond resigns as First Minister of Scotland in November 2014

When the United States were formed and the thirteen states selected their first governors, nine were of Scottish ancestry. Remarkably, all the members of the first American Cabinet had Scottish ancestry.

53. Sir JAMES YOUNG SIMPSON (1811 – 1870)

KEY POINTS:

- Born in Bathgate near Edinburgh, the son of a baker.
- Professor of Midwifery at Edinburgh University.
- He pioneered the use of anaesthesia, particularly chloroform, developing its function in surgery and midwifery. In November, 1847, chloroform was first used to relieve pain during childbirth. The first child born under chloroform was christened Anaesthesia.
- Chloroform (inhalable anaesthetic) was administered to Queen Victoria as a pain relief for the births of her two children, Prince Leopold (in 1853) and Princess Beatrice (in 1857) Thereafter its use became generally accepted. Chloroform was on its way to becoming the most widely used general anaesthetic.

Figure 53 (a):
Sir James Young Simpson
(Courtesy Royal College of Physicians of Edinburgh)

- Honours were heaped on Simpson. Queen Victoria made him a baronet in 1886.
- His family was offered a resting place for him in Westminster Abbey but his wife declined the offer.
- See figures: 53 (a) & (b)

Figure 53 (b): The moment of discovery of the anaesthetic properties of chloroform by James Young Simpson and his two assistants. After they have inhaled the vapour, Simpson is on his knees, and the assistants on the floor/asleep at the table. The memorable moment was witnessed by Simpson's wife and others.
(Illustrated by Duncan Galbraith, Tayinloan, Argyll)

54.   Sir WALTER SCOTT (1771 – 1832)

KEY POINTS:

- Born in Edinburgh.
- Studied law at Edinburgh University.
- His first novel *Waverley*, published in 1814, became an international bestseller. Other works include *Ivanhoe*, *Rob Roy*, and *The Lady of the Lake*.
- His poetry, novels and style placed him in the romantic movement of 19th century Europe. The picture of the romantic highland hero that he created produced an image of Scotland the world over.
- In 1822 he organised George IV's Edinburgh visit. When he went to greet the King, *"Ah"* exclaimed the King, dressed in the kilt, *"Walter Scott, the man I most wanted to see"*. The visit of the King was an extravaganza of highland culture that helped establish tartan as the national dress of Scotland.
- In recognition of Sir Walter Scott, prominent statues are in Princes Street, Edinburgh and George Square, Glasgow.
- Scott has been honoured by appearing on the front of the banknotes issued by the Bank of Scotland.
- Scott was an astute businessman and struggled throughout his career to stop 'pirated' editions of his works. He was largely unsuccessful in this, much to his chagrin.
- See figures: 54 (a), (b), (c) and (d)

Figure 54 (b): The Scott Monument on Princess St, Edinburgh

Figure 54 (a):
Scott Monument in
George Square, Glasgow

Figure 54 (c):
Monument to George IVs
Edinburgh visit in 1822, in
George Street, Edinburgh

Figure 54 (d): Bank of Scotland launched banknotes featuring Sir Walter Scott in their Tercentenary Series (1995) and Bridges Series (2007) *(Courtesy Bank of Scotland)*

55. MARY SLESSOR (1848 – 1915)

KEY POINTS:

- Born in Aberdeen and lived in Dundee.
- Mary Slessor had fiery red hair.
- She worked in a textile mill in Dundee.
- Mary asked her mother: *"What's it like in Africa?"* Her mother answered: *"Many people in Africa don't know that God sent his only son Jesus into this world to save them from sin."*
- In 1876 at the age of 27 she joined the Calabar Mission in West Africa as a Christian missionary. Known as *"The White Queen of Obkoyong"*.
- Mary died on 13th January, 1915, amongst the people she loved and the country she called home - AFRICA.
- Clydesdale Bank issued the £10 banknote in May 1997 in her memory, in the Famous Scots Series.
- See figures: 55 (a), (b) & (c)

Figure 55 (a):
Memorial to Mary Slessor, Steeple
Church, Dundee
(Photograph: Heather Soutar, Dundee)

Figure 55 (b):
This stained glass window shows Mary Slessor with African
children in the café of the McManus Museum, Dundee
(Photograph: Heather Soutar, Dundee)

Figure 55 (c):
Front: Mary Slessor, the missionary in
West Africa
(Courtesy Clydesdale Bank)

56.   ADAM SMITH (1723 – 1790)

KEY POINTS:

- Born in Kirkcaldy.
- An economist and philosopher.
- Professor of Moral Philosophy at Glasgow University.
- Wrote the famous book *The Wealth of Nations* - the foundation of modern economic thinking.
- He has been rightly called the Father of Political Economy.
- Smith believed in the benefits of free trade between nations and that economies would prosper through competition. Ironically, Smith's hard-nosed support of materialistic capitalism is underpinned by the metaphysical Christian idea of providence, common in the 18th century.
- Elected Lord Rector of Glasgow University.
- In 1981 Clydesdale Bank launched a £50 banknote featuring Adam Smith in the Famous Scots Series.
- Died on 17th July, 1790 and was buried in the Cannongate churchyard, Edinburgh.
- See figures: 56 (a), (b) & (c)

Figure 56 (a): Front: Adam Smith the economist
and author of *The Wealth of Nations*
(Courtesy Clydesdale Bank)

Figure 56 (b): A
commemorative
plaque for Adam
Smith in Kirkcaldy

Figure 56 (c): Monument to Adam Smith in
High Street, Edinburgh

57. JOHN SMITH (1938 – 1994)

KEY POINTS:

- Born in Dalmally in Argyll.
- Brought up in Islay for the first two years of his life, then in Ardrishaig.
- Graduated from Glasgow University MA, LLB.
- He became leader of the Labour Party in July 1992, giving his heart and soul to the Labour Party.
- One of the best loved and most admired Scotsmen. Yet he did not find favour among the prime movers of the 'New Labour' movement, who felt that he looked more like a bank manager than a leader of a great political party.
- He died of a heart attack on 12th May, 1994 at the height of his political career.
- The last public words from John Smith on the night before his death were: *"We will do our best to reward your faith in us but please give us the opportunity to serve our country. That is all we ask".*
- He is buried in the Island of Iona, one of the main centres of Christianity, where in AD 653 St Columba landed from Ireland to bring Christianity to Scotland.
- See figure 57

Figure 57: John Smith's gravestone in the graveyard at Iona Abbey

58. ROBERT LOUIS STEVENSON (1850 – 1894)

KEY POINTS:

- Born in Edinburgh into a family of lighthouse builders.
- Graduated from Edinburgh University with a degree in law, but hardly practised.
- Was a prolific writer of fiction, non-fiction and poetry.
- Wrote two classic Scottish novels *Kidnapped* and *The Master of Ballantrae* as well as *A Child's Garden of Verses, The Strange Case of Dr Jekyll and Mr Hyde* and *Treasure Island. The Strange Case of Dr Jekyll and Mr Hyde* became one of the best-selling works of fiction of the time. Treasure Island is remembered for some of its characters such as *Long John Silver.*
- Some of his novels had been adapted into films. *Dr Jekyll and Mr Hyde* was made into a live action film by Walt Disney. Dr Jekyll has a very distinguished Hollywood history. Silent adaptations were made in the early 20th century, and acclaimed interpretations of the novel – starring Frederic March and Spencer Tracy respectively – were made in the 1930s and 1940s.
- He settled in Samoa and died there in 1894, aged only 44 years.
- See figures: 58 (a), (b) & (c)

Figure 58 (a): Robert Louis Stevenson

Figure 58 (b): Robert Louis Stevenson appeared on the front of the £1 note issued by The Royal Bank of Scotland
(Courtesy The Royal Bank of Scotland)

Figure 58 (c): Monument to Robert Louis Stevenson, Colinton Parish Church of Scotland, Edinburgh
(Photograph: Dr David Williamson)

59. Sir JACKIE STEWART (1939 – Present)

KEY POINTS:

- Born in Milton in Dunbartonshire.
- Educated at Dumbarton Academy.
- Became a professional motor racing driver.
- He retired from Formula One motor racing at the end of 1973 after winning three World Championships and 27 Grands Prix during a nine-year career.
- Became an outspoken advocate for auto racing safety. Campaigned for improved emergency services and better safety barriers around race tracks.
- He was a play-by-play announcer for the 1976 Winter Olympics and the 1976 Summer Olympics.
- Honours: In 1996, awarded an honorary doctorate by Heriot Watt University in Edinburgh; in 2008 awarded an honorary Doctor of Science (D.Sc.) degree from the University of St Andrews and many others.
- He helped to introduce road safety as part of the school curriculum.
- He was knighted in 2001 for services to motor racing.
- See figure 59

Figure 59: Jackie Stewart in his motor racing car
(Courtesy Dumbarton Library, Dumbarton)

60. WILLIAM ALEXANDER SMITH (1854 – 1914)

KEY POINTS:

Figure 60: Logo of the Boys' Brigade

- Born in Thurso, Scotland.
- Founder of the Boys' Brigade Company, complete with military-style uniform, army-style discipline and leadership structure. His idea of the Boys' Brigade soon caught on and companies were formed throughout Scotland, and the Boy's Brigade is now active across the world.
- See figure 60

61. NICOLA STURGEON (1970 – Present)

KEY POINTS:

Figure 61 (a): Nicola Sturgeon

- Born in Ayrshire on 19th July, 1970.
- Graduated Bachelor of Laws (Hons) in 1992, with a Diploma in Legal Practice the following year.
- Worked as a solicitor in Glasgow.
- Joined the Scottish National Party (SNP) in 1986.
- She is the fifth and current First Minister of Scotland and the Leader of the Scottish National Party. In office since 2014. She is the first woman to hold either position.
- A high- profile figure in Scottish politics. Most popular leader in the UK.
- She won the Scottish Politician of the Year Award in 2008, 2012 and 2014. In 2004, 2008 and 2011 she also won the Donald Dewar Debater of the Year Award.
- Sturgeon is representative of a trend within Scottish politics towards leaders who are neither male nor especially charismatic. The benefits and drawbacks of this very recent development remain to be seen.
- See figures: 61 (a) & (b)

Figure 61 (b): Nicola Sturgeon (front right) with former leader Alex Salmond and the rest of the Scottish Cabinet following election in 2011.

62. THOMAS TELFORD (1757 – 1834)

KEY POINTS:
- Telford was born in Eskdale in Dumfriesshire.
- *He became one of the greatest architects and civil engineers in British history, building a plethora of roads, canals and bridges. A master bridge builder.*
- Thomas Telford's masterpiece was the sixty miles long Caledonian Canal, between Inverness and Fort William. He was also famous for building the Menai suspension bridge.
- He was a Fellow of the Royal Society of Edinburgh and London.
- Telford was a lifelong bachelor and died at the age of 77.
- See figure 62

63. WILLIAM THOMSON - Lord KELVIN (1824 – 1907)

KEY POINTS:
- Born in Belfast but moved to Glasgow at the age of eight.
- A 19th century physicist.
- Professor of Natural Philosophy at Glasgow University.
- Internationally famous for his work on thermodynamics.
- He gave his name to the Kelvin scale, the internationally recognised scale of absolute temperature. Zero, known as absolute zero, is the lowest possible temperature, never in practice achievable.
- He was awarded a peerage, taking the title Lord Kelvin of Largs.
- In 1971 Clydesdale Bank issued a £100 banknote featuring Lord Kelvin in the Famous Scots Series.
- See figures: 63 (a) & (b)

Figure 63 (a): Front: Lord Kelvin
the researcher and inventor
(Courtesy Clydesdale Bank)

Figure 63 (b):
Statue of Lord Kelvin
in Kelvingrove Park,
Glasgow

Figure 62: Monument to Thomas Telford at
Clydeport Authority, Robertson Street, Glasgow.
His contribution to the development of the Clyde
is recognised in this monument in which Telford
is holding technical plans under his left arm.

64. JAMES YOUNG (1811 – 1883)

KEY POINTS:

- Born in Glasgow.
- Attended Andersonian University, now the University of Strathclyde, Glasgow.
- He developed the process of refining oil from shale coal.
- Realised that oil will burn easily and produce a bright light.
- He called the oil paraffin oil. It is used for lighting and cooking.
- *He financially supported David Livingstone's expedition to Africa.*
- He was elected Fellow of the Royal Society and awarded an Honorary LLD by St Andrews University.
- He went on to set up Scotland's oil industry.
- See figure 64

Figure 64:
A Lantern (Paraffin Oil Lamp)

65. JAMES WATT (1736 – 1819)

KEY POINTS:

- Born in Greenock on the Clyde in 1736.
- Strictly speaking, James Watt did not invent the steam engine, but redesigned it and improved its efficiency. He patented it in 1769.
- In 1782 Watt invented a double action engine that further improved the efficiency and power of the engine. He originated the concept of horsepower and introduced the term "horsepower". Watt (W) was adopted as a standard measurement of power or work done per unit of time.
- His invention proved to be the breakthrough in harnessing the power of steam for industrial use, accelerating the industrial revolution. Without Watt's steam engine, the age of the railway would not have arrived.
- He received many honours. He was a Fellow of the Royal Societies of Edinburgh and London. He was granted an honorary LLD from the University of Glasgow. He was offered a baronetcy which he gracefully declined.
- See figure 65

Figure 65:
Monument to James Watt in George Square, Glasgow

66. Sir ROBERT WATSON WATT (1892 – 1978)

KEY POINTS:

- Born in Brechin, Angus.
- Graduated from Dundee University with a degree in engineering.
- Worked as a meteorologist and became fascinated by radio waves.
- In 1923 succeeded in discovering the science underlying radar technology.
- On 26th February 1935, he gave the first practical demonstration of high frequency radar for the purpose of aircraft detection. The invention of radar made an invaluable contribution to the Battle of Britain with Germany in the Second World War.
- Radar came to be a vital part of the world's transport and communication network.
- Eventually radar was in routine use around the world for air traffic control and navigational aid and for catching speeding motorists.
- See figures: 66 (a), (b) & (c)

Figure 66 (a): Robert Watson Watt
(Courtesy of Angus Archives, Copyright Angus Council)

Figure 66 (b): Chain home radar tower (transmitter mast), Lincolnshire, Wolds at Stenigot
(Courtesy of Owen Rushby)

Figure 66 (c): Radar head on top of the Air Traffic Tower, Cairo, Egypt
(Courtesy Jim Rogers, Helensburgh, Argyll)

67. TOM WEIR (1914 – 2004)

KEY POINTS:

- Born in Springburn, Glasgow.
- Tom was a self-made man.
- For about four decades he wrote with considerable passion for *The Scots Magazine* under the title 'My Month', showing his enchantment with Scotland, its people and wildlife.
- He hosted the very popular television programme *Weir's Way*. He was Scottish Television Personality of the Year in 1978, and in 2000, received the inaugural John Muir Lifetime Achievement Award.
- Tom was an explorer, climber, writer and photographer.
- See figure 67

Figure 67: Monument to Tom Weir at Balmaha, Stirlingshire

68. WILLIAM WALLACE (c.1270 – 1305)

KEY POINTS:

- It is thought that he was born south of Glasgow in Elderslie, Renfrewshire, the son of a small landowner.
- William Wallace was the ultimate inspiration, the leader the Scottish people looked up to. He did not disappoint them.
- There were two main driving forces in his life (a) a firm belief in freedom for his countrymen and (b) an absolute hatred of English oppression. Defeated an English army at the Battle of Stirling in 1297.
- William Wallace is a hero the Scots can be well and truly proud of. The figure of William Wallace looms large in Scottish history just as his famous monument dominates the skyline at Stirling.
- His fame gained a new lease of life in 1995 with the release of the Hollywood film *Braveheart*, a popular retelling of the Scottish struggle for independence. Mel Gibson directed and starred as William Wallace. The film won five Oscars.
- Inside the Wallace Monument, there is the Hall of Heroes containing busts of sixteen well known Scots. The busts are of:
  Sir David Brewster (1781-1868), scientist and inventor; Robert the Bruce (1724-1329), King of Scotland and national hero; George Buchanan (1506-1582), historian and scholar; Robert Burns (1759-1796), poet; Thomas Carlyle (1795-1881), writer and sage; Thomas Chalmers (1780-1847), preacher and writer; William Ewart Gladstone (1809-1898), politician and UK prime minister; John Knox (1512-1572), religious reformer; David Livingstone (1813-1873), missionary and explorer; Hugh Miller (1802-1856), writer and geologist; William Murdock (1754-1839), pioneer of gas lighting; Allan Ramsay (1686-1758), poet; Sir Walter Scott (1771-18320, writer, poet and nationalist; Adam Smith (1723-1790), economist and philosopher; Robert Tannahill (1774-1810, songwriter; James Watt (1736-1819), inventor and developer of the steam engine.
- See figure 68

Figure 68: Wallace Monument, Stirling
(Photograph: John Broadfoot, Stirling)

FAMOUS SCOTS AND SCIENTIFIC TERMS

Alexander Graham Bell
- Decibel (dB): To measure hearing response and compare with standard hearing curves.

Robert Brown
- Brownian Movement/Motion: Is the random motion of particles suspended in a fluid (a liquid or a gas) resulting from their collision with the quick atoms or molecules in the gas or liquid.

James Clerk Maxwell
- Maxwell's Rule/Equations: Maxwell's equations describe how electric and magnetic fields are generated and altered by each other and by charges and currents.

Thomas Graham
- Graham's Laws of Diffusion and Effusion:
  Diffusion – The rate at which two gases mix.
  Graham's Law of Diffusion: The rate at which gases diffuse is inversely proportional to the square root of their densities.
  Effusion- The rate at which a gas escapes through a pinhole into a vacuum.
  Graham's Law of Effusion: The rate of effusion of a gas is inversely proportional to the square root of either the density or the molar mass of the gas.

James Watt
- Watt
  The watt (Abbreviated W) is the International system of Units (SI) standard unit of power (energy per unit time). One Watt equals one joule per second. 1 W= 1volt –ampere; 746= 1 horsepower (hp).

Lord Kelvin
- Kelvin:
  The Kelvin is a unit of measure for temperature based upon an absolute scale. The Kelvin scale is an absolute thermodynamic temperature scale using as its null point absolute zero and is assigned the unit symbol K.

Other Great Scots categorised according to SURNAME (Alphabetical by Surname)

No.	First Name	Surname	Birthplace	Born/Died	Profession/Contribution
1	Robert	Adam	Kirkcaldy	1728-1792	Architect of Georgian Britain. His work includes Culzean Castle, Hopetoun House and Charlotte Square in Edinburgh.
2	William	Adam	Linktown of Abbotshall, Fife	1689-1748	Foremost architect of his time.
3	Robert	Adamson	Burnside, Fife	1821-1848	Scottish chemist and photographer.
4	John	Aitken	Falkirk	1839-1919	Scottish physicist and meteorologist. Discovered the crucial role that microscopic particles play in the condensation of atmospheric water vapour in clouds and fogs. Now known as Aitken nuclei.
5	Sir William	Allan	Edinburgh	1782-1850	Scottish historical painter
6	Ronnie	Ancona	Troon	1968-	Named best TV Comedy Actress at the 2003 British Comedy Awards.
7	Arthur	Anderson	Shetland	1792-1868	Set up the Peninsular and Oriental Steam Navigation Company, known today as P&O Ferries.
8	Moira	Anderson	Kirkintilloch	1938-	Singer.
9	Tom	Anderson	Shetland	1910-1991	Fiddler, composer and folklorist. Awarded an MBE.
10	John	Arbuthnot	Inverbervie	1667-1735	Scottish mathematician, physician and satirist.
11	Sir William	Arrol	Houston, Renfrewshire	1839-1913	Engineer, famous for Tay Railway Bridge and Forth Railway Bridge. Knighted in 1890.
12	Margot (Countess of Oxford and Asquith)	Asquith	Peeblesshire (Tweedsdale)	1864-1945	Anglo-Scottish socialite, author and wit.
13	Katherine Marjory	Atholl	Alyth, Perthshire	1864-1960	First Scottish woman Member of Parliament; first woman cabinet minister at the Department of Education.
14	Tim	Baillie	Aberdeen	1979-	Scottish slalom canoer; claimed Britain's first ever canoe slalom gold at the London Olympics.

No.	First Name	Surname	Birthplace	Born/Died	Profession/Contribution
15	Aly	Bain	Lerwick, Shetland Islands	1946-	Folk musician, awarded an MBE.
16	Alexander	Bain	Caithness	1810-1877	Watchmaker, patented the world's first electric clock in 1841. Best remembered for inventing one of the earliest fax machines, a device which scanned and transmitted images. Awarded the technology and engineering Emmy for designing the concept of scanning for image transmission, which was used in the development of television. (See figure 69)
17	Magnus Macfarlane	Barrow	Dalmally, Argyll	1968-	Set up the charity, Mary's Meals, helping to feed the world's hungry children.
18	Stanley	Baxter	Glasgow	1926-	Scottish actor and impressionist, known for his popular British television comedy shows.
19	Jim	Baxter	Hill of Beath, Fife	1939-2001	Gifted footballer.
20	Sir George Thomas	Beatson	Trincomalee, Sri Lanka	1848-1933	Famous oncologist. Beatson West of Scotland Cancer Centre Glasgow is named in his honour.
21	Sir George	Beilby	Edinburgh	1850-1924	Scottish industrial chemist.
22	Sir Charles	Bell	Edinburgh	1774-1842	Author of The Nervous System of the Human Body. Scottish anatomist. Knighted in 1831.
23	Ian	Bell	Portobello	1956-2015	Scottish columnist, respected across politics.
24	Nicola	Benedetti	Irvine, Ayrshire	1987-	Classical violinist.
25	Joseph	Black	Bordeaux in France, Black's father was from a Scottish family who settled in Belfast, his mother was from Aberdeenshire.	1728-1799	The father of modern chemistry. Discovered carbon dioxide (CO_2), the concept of specific and latent heat.
26	Elizabeth	Blackadder	Falkirk	1931-	Scottish painter; first Scottish woman painter elected to full membership of Royal Academy (1976) and Royal Scottish Academy (1972). Awarded an OBE in 1982.

No.	First Name	Surname	Birthplace	Born/Died	Profession/Contribution
27	Sir Charles (Chay)	Blyth	Hawick	1940-	Sailor; the first person to sail single-handed, non-stop, around the world. Knighted in 1997.
28	Sir Robert	Boothby	Edinburgh	1900-1986	Scottish Conservative politician.
29	James	Boswell	Edinburgh	1740-1795	Biographer, wrote Dr Samuel Johnson's biography. Writer and journalist.
30	Susan	Boyle	Blackburn, West Lothian	1961-	Singer.
31	James	Braid	Portmoak, Kinross-shire	1795-1860	Regarded by many as the first genuine hypnotherapist and the father of modern hypnotism.
32	James	Braidwood	Edinburgh	1800-1861	Father of the British Fire Service. Founder of the world's first municipal fire service in Edinburgh in 1824 and first director of the London Fire Brigade. (See figure 70)
33	Sir David	Brewster	Jedburgh, Scottish Borders	1781-1868	Invented the Kaleidoscope: in 1815. His initial design was a tube with pairs of mirrors at one end, pairs of translucent discs at the other, and beads between the two. Initially intended as a scientific tool, the kaleidoscope was later copied as a toy.(See figures:71 A & B)
34	Sir Thomas	Brisbane	Largs, Ayrshire	1773-1860	Governor of New South Wales (Australia) (1821-1825). A new convict settlement was named after him and became today's city of Brisbane.
35	John	Broadwood	Born at St Helens, Cockburnspath in Berwickshire but grew up in East Lothian	1732-1812	Made the first grand piano, Scottish founder of the piano manufacturer Broadwood and Sons.
36	Henry Peter (1st Baron Brougham and vaux)	Brougham	Cowgate, Edinburgh	1778-1868	British statesman who became Lord Chancellor of Great Britain.
37	Robert	Brown	Montrose, near Aberdeen	1773-1858	Identified the nucleus in living cells. Noted movement of fine particles in a liquid, named the Brownian Movement/ Motion.
38	John	Brown	Craithenaird, Balmoral	1826-1883	Ghillie on the Royal estate at Balmoral and personal attendant of Queen Victoria. In 1997 the film Mrs Brown was released based on the story of John Brown and Queen Victoria. starring Billy Connolly and Judi Dench.

No.	First Name	Surname	Birthplace	Born/Died	Profession/Contribution
39	George	Brown	Glasgow	1818-1880	Journalist and politician, emigrated to Canada in 1843 and known as the founding father of Canada.
40	Janet	Brown	Rutherglen, Glasgow	1923-	Scottish actress, comedienne and impressionist. Best known for her lampoons of prime minister Margaret Thatcher, to whom she bore a superficial physical resemblance.
41	Thomas	Bruce	Broomhall, Fife	1766-1841	7th Earl Elgin & Kincardine. Brought the Elgin Marbles from Greece. Now in the British Museum. (See figure 72)
42	Sir David	Bruce	Born in Australia to Scottish parents	1855-1931	Microbiologist, identified the cause of African trypanosomiasis (sleeping sickness). Brucellosis is named after him.
43	James	Bruce	Kinnaird, Stirlingshire	1730-1794	Explorer and travel writer.
44	William Spiers	Bruce	London	1867-1921	Scottish naturalist, polar scientist and oceanographer.
45	Sir James	Brunlees	A native of Kelso	1816-1892	Laid the first railway line across the Alps, Scottish Civil Engineer.
46	Bill	Bryden	Greenock	1942-	Stage director and dramatist. Awarded a CBE in 1993.
47	John	Buchan	Perth	1857-1940	Author and Statesman. Governor General of Canada, Chancellor of Edinburgh University, biographer and politician, Lord High Commissioner to the General Assembly of the Church of Scotland in 1933. Best known for his thriller *The 39 Steps*, filmed by Hitchcock in 1935.
48	William	Buchan	Ancrum, Roxburghshire	1729-1805	Wrote *Domestic Medicine or The Family Physician*. 19 English editions were published during his lifetime.
49	Ken	Buchanan	Edinburgh	1945-	Boxer. Undisputed World Light Heavyweight Champion.
50	Jack	Buchanan	Helensburgh	1891-1957	Theatre and film actor, dancer, producer and director.
51	Sir Matt	Busby	Bellshill, Lanarkshire	1909-1994	Football manager, knighted for his services to sport.
52	Gerard	Butler	Paisley	1969-	Film and TV singer and actor.
53	John	Byrne	Paisley	1940-	Scottish dramatist and stage designer. Awarded an MBE in 2001.

No.	First Name	Surname	Birthplace	Born/ Died	Profession/Contribution
54	Thomas	Campbell	Glasgow	1777-1844	One of Britain's most popular poets, Rector of Glasgow University. (See figure 73)
55	Nicholas Andrew Argyll (Nicky)	Campbell	Edinburgh	1961-	Journalist, radio and TV presenter.
56	Sir Walter (Menzies)	Campbell	Glasgow	1941-	Advocate and former Liberal Democratic Party leader.
57	Sir Colin	Campbell- Lord Clyde of Clydesdale	Glasgow	1792-1863	Made a Field Marshall.
58	Sir James	Cantlie	Banffshire	1856-1926	Physician and pioneer of first aid.
59	Robert	Carlyle	Glasgow	1961-	One of the better British actors of his generation.
60	Willie	Carson	Stirling	1942-	Scottish jockey. First Scotsman to be champion jockey.
61	Rev. Donald	Carson		1902-1983	Helped British servicemen flee occupied France.
62	Thomas	Chalmers	Anstruther, Fife	1780-1847	Scotland's greatest 19th century churchman. Led a third of the Church of Scotland ministers to form the Free Church.
63	James	Chalmers	Arbroath	1782-1853	Inventor of the adhesive postage stamp.
64	William	Chambers	Peebles	1800-1883	Scottish publisher.
65	Ian	Charleston	Edinburgh	1949-1990	Actor; played Olympian Eric Liddell in the Oscar Winning Chariots of Fire film.
66	Bonnie Prince	Charlie	Born in Italy – Grandson of James VII of Scotland and II of England	1720-1788	Led the ill-fated Jacobite Rebellion of 1745. The young pretender to the throne of Great Britain. (See figure 74)
67	Philip	Christison	Edinburgh	1893-1993	Scottish general WW2 and ornithologist.
68	Jim	Clark	Kilmany, Fife	1936-1968	Formula One racing driver.
69	Sir Dugald	Clerk	Glasgow	1854-1932	Scottish mechanical engineer. In 1881 patented a gas engine working on the two stroke principle known as the Clerk cycle. Knighted in 1917.

No.	First Name	Surname	Birthplace	Born/Died	Profession/Contribution
70	Dr George	Cleghorn	Granton, near Edinburgh	1716-1789	Helped discover Quinine as cure for Malaria.
71	Ralph	Cochrane	Springfield, Fife	1895-1977	Scottish Air Chief Marshal.
72	Thomas	Cochrane	Annesfield, Lanarkshire	1775-1860	Scottish naval commander. One of Britain's greatest seamen. Buried in Westminster Abbey.
73	William	Collins	Eastwood, Renfrewshire	1789-1853	Book publisher; a major publisher of Bibles.
74	Robbie	Coltrane	Rutherglen	1950-	Actor and comedian.
75	Archibald	Constable	Carnbee, Fife	1774-1827	A Scottish publisher, bookseller and stationer.
76	Robin	Cook	Bellshill	1946-2005	Scottish Labour politician. Became Leader of House of Commons in 2001, quit in protest over war in Iraq. Died on walking holiday in north west Scotland.
77	Ronnie	Corbett	Edinburgh	1930-2016	Scottish comedian and actor. Successful partnership with Ronnie Barker led to *The Two Ronnies* (1971-87).
78	Daniel	Cotter	Glasgow	1838-1891	Stained glass artist, designer, interior decorator and art dealer.
79	David	Coulthard	Twynholm, near Dumfries	1971-	Formula One racing driver.
80	Archibald Scott	Couper	Kirkintilloch	1831-1892	Scottish chemist who proposed an early theory of chemical structure and bonding. Developed the concept of tetravalent carbon atoms linking together to form large molecules and that the bonding order of atoms in a molecule can be determined from chemical evidence. To him chemistry was a philosophy the end of which was theory.
81	Thomas	Coutts	Edinburgh	1735-1822	One of Scotland's shrewdest money makers. Anglo-Scottish banker. Founder of Coutts & Co, London.
82	Sir John James	Cowperthwaite	Edinburgh	1915-2006	Financial Secretary of Hong Kong; introduced free market economic policies, turning post-war Hong Kong into a thriving global financial centre.
83	Brian	Cox	Dundee	1946-	First actor to play the infamous Hannibal Lecter (in the 1987 film *Manhunter*).

No.	First Name	Surname	Birthplace	Born/ Died	Profession/Contribution
84	James	Craig	Edinburgh	1739-1795	Architect, remembered primarily for his layout of the first Edinburgh New Town.
85	James	Craik	Arbigland, Scotland	1730-1814	Organised the medical services of Washington's Army. Physician General of the United States Army.
86	Robert (Bob)	Crampsey	Glasgow	1930-2008	Teacher and broadcaster.
87	Kate	Cranston	Glasgow	1849-1934	Leading figure in the development of tea rooms (Miss Cranston's Tea Rooms).
88	Sir Alexander	Crichton	Edinburgh	1763-1856	Physician to Emperor of Russia in 1803; author.
89	Donald	Crisp	London	1882-1974	Actor. Won an Academy Award for best supporting actor in 1942 for his performance in *How Green is my Valley*.
90	Annette	Crosbie	Gorebridge, Midlothian	1934-	Highly acclaimed actress.
91	Alexander	Cruden	Aberdeen	1699-1770	Author of the famous Bible's concordance, Cruden's Complete Concordance.
92	Andrew	Cruickshank	Aberdeen	1907-1988	Actor- Dr Finlay's Casebook.
93	Alan	Cumming	Aberfeldy	1965-	Actor, singer, director, producer and TV presenter
94	Sir Alan Gordon	Cunningham	Dublin, Ireland	1887-1983	Senior officer in the British army during the second world war. High Commissioner of Palestine.
95	Robert	Cunninghame-Graham	London	1852-1936	Politician, first President of the newly formed Scottish Labour Party, later becoming President of the National Party of Scotland (1928) and the Scottish National Party (1934).
96	David	Dale	Stewarton, Ayrshire	1739-1806	Set up Scotland's first cotton mill and the mills at New Lanark.
97	Kenny	Dalglish	Glasgow	1951-	Scottish football player and manager.
98	Sir Hugh	Dalrymple Lord Drummond	East Lothian	1700-1753	Invented better drainage system for agriculture, hollow pipe drainage.
99	William Denny* & brothers	Denny (brothers)	Dumbarton	1779-1833*	Scottish shipbuilding company. Built over 1500 ships from 1844 to 1963 including Cutty Sark. (See figure 75)
100	Barbara	Dickson	Dunfermline	1947-	Singer.

No.	First Name	Surname	Birthplace	Born/Died	Profession/Contribution
101	Tommy	Docherty	Glasgow	1928-	Footballer and manager.
102	Donovan Philips Leitch	Donovan	Maryhill, Glasgow	1946-	Scottish singer, songwriter and guitarist. Friend of The Beatles
103	Sir Alec	Douglas-Home	London	1903-1995	British conservative politician, Prime Minister (1963-1964). Prided himself on being Scottish but was educated at Eton and Oxford.
104	Sir John Sholto (9th Marquess of Queensberry)	Douglas	Florence, Italy	1844-1900	Devised the Queensberry Rules for Boxing in 1867.
105	Hugh(1st Baron Dowding)	Dowding	Moffat, Scotland	1882-1970	Air Chief Marshall.
106	Thomas	Drummond	Edinburgh	1797-1840	Drummond light. (See figure 76)
107	Dame Carol Ann	Duffy	Glasgow	1955-	Scottish poet and playwright. Appointed Britain's Poet Laureate in 2009.
108	Rev. Henry	Duncan	Lochrutton, Kirkcudbrightshire	1774-1846	Scottish minister, geologist and social reformer. Founder of the world's first commercial savings bank.
109	Adam (1st Viscount Duncan)	Duncan	Dundee	1731-1804	British admiral who defeated the Dutch fleet off Camperdown. Victory was considered one of the most significant actions in naval history.
110	Henry (1st Viscount Melville)	Dundas	Amiston, Midlothian	1742-1811	Scottish advocate and politician. He is commemorated by one of the most prominent memorials in Edinburgh in St Andrew Square.
111	Douglas	Dunn	Inchinnan, Renfrewshire	1942-	Scottish poet, academic and critic.
112	Sheena	Easton	Bellshill, Glasgow	1959-	Pop singer and actress.
113	John (6th Earl of Mar)	Erskine	Scotland	1675-1732	Scottish Jacobite.
114	Sir William	Fairbairn	A native of Kelso	1789-1874	Scottish engineer. Advised government on the use of iron for defensive purposes. Built the Conway and Menai tubular bridges in 1845. The first iron–hulled steamship. Elected FRS in 1850, made a baronet in 1869.
115	William Ronald Dodds	Fairbairn	Edinburgh	1889-1964	Psychiatrist and psychoanalyst who had a profound influence on early psychoanalysis.

No.	First Name	Surname	Birthplace	Born/ Died	Profession/Contribution
116	Sir Tom	Farmer	Leith	1940-	Scottish businessman and philanthropist. Set up Kwik-Fit.
117	Sir Alex	Ferguson	Govan, Glasgow	1941-	Former manager of Manchester United Football Club.
118	Adam	Ferguson	Logierait in Atholl, Perthshire	1723-1816	Scottish philosopher and historian of the Scottish Enlightenment.
119	Craig	Ferguson	Glasgow	1962-	Scottish stand-up comedian, writer and actor. Currently one of North America's highest earning Chat Show hosts.
120	Robert	Fergusson	Edinburgh	1750-1774	A Scottish poet. Published *Auld Reekie* in 1773, now regarded as his masterpiece. A vivid verse portrait of his home city intended as the first part of a planned long poem. Despite a short life, his career was highly influential, especially through his impact on Robert Burns. (See figure 77)
121	Sir Bernard	Fergusson	British born	1911-1980	Last British born Governor General of New Zealand.
122	Sheila	Fleet	Born in Orkney	1945-	Jewellery designer. Manufactures in Orkney, Scotland. Awarded an OBE in 2013.
123	Williamina	Fleming	Dundee	1857-1911	Scottish astronomer.
124	Duncan (Lord Culloden)	Forbes	Near Inverness	1685-1747	Lord President of the Court of Session.
125	Bill	Forsyth	Glasgow	1946-	Director, writer and producer of films.
126	Sir Hugh (2nd Baron Fraser of Allander)	Fraser	Bearsden	1936-1987	Erstwhile chairman of House of Fraser, Harrods, George Outram and Whyte & Mackay.
127	Ian	Frazer	Glasgow	1953-	Known for the creation of the human papillomavirus vaccine.
128	Sir James George	Frazer	Glasgow	1854-1941	Cultural anthropologist and founding father of modern anthropology. His most famous work, *The Golden Bough*, contained in its original form criticisms of Christianity deemed unsuitable for publication until the 1980s.
129	Rikki	Fulton	Glasgow	1924-2004	Comedian, actor and entertainer.
130	Will	Fyffe	Dundee	1885-1947	Film star and music hall artiste of the 30s and 40s.

No.	First Name	Surname	Birthplace	Born/Died	Profession/Contribution
131	Willie	Gallacher	Paisley	1881-1965	Communist politician.
132	John	Galt	Irvine	1779-1839	Author, explorer.
133	Mary	Garden	Aberdeen	1874-1967	Opera Singer.
134	Kathleen	Garscadden	Glasgow	1897-1991	Worked as a presenter, broadcaster and producer for 42 years on the series *Children's Hour*.
135	Sir Patrick	Geddes	Perth	1854-1933	One of the modern pioneers of the concept of town and country planning.
136	Archibald	Geikie	Edinburgh	1835-1924	Scottish Geologist. Elected FRS at the age of 29 and knighted in 1909.
137	Sir Alexander	Gibson	Motherwell	1926-1995	Founded Scottish Opera in 1962, musician, conductor.
138	Dr Marion	Gilchrist	Bothwell, South Lanarkshire	1864-1952	First woman to graduate as a medic from a Scottish university and a leading suffragette.
139	A.A.	Gill	Edinburgh	1954-	Newspaper columnist and writer
140	Sir David	Gill	Aberdeen	1843-1914	Scottish astronomer. Knighted in 1900.
141	John	Glaister	Lanark	1856-1932	GP, police surgeon and Scottish forensic scientist.
142	Evelyn	Glennie	Aberdeen	1965-	Solo percussionist.
143	Thomas Blake	Glover	Fraseburgh, Aberdeenshire	1838-1911	He was known as the "Scottish Samurai" who risked everything to travel from Aberdeen to the Japanese city of Nagasaki during the 19th century. As one of the founders of the Mitsubishi Corporation, now Japan's largest general trading company, Glover gained fame in Japan. He is credited with helping to start Japan's industrial revolution. In 1908 he was awarded the Order of the Rising Sun. He provided the first ships for the Japanese navy, built the country's first railways, established the first mint and introduced coal mining. Glover's Japanese home survived the atom bomb and has become a tourist attraction.

No.	First Name	Surname	Birthplace	Born/ Died	Profession/Contribution
144	Sir Alexander	Gordon	Strathbraan, Perthshire	1752-1799	Performed the first epidemiological study of puerperal fever, the contagious and transmissible nature of the condition and its avoidance.
145	Hannah	Gordon	Edinburgh	1941-	Scottish actress.
146	Neil	Gow	Dunkeld	1727-1807	The most famous Scottish fiddler and dancie (travelling bard and dance instructor).
147	Dr Thomas	Graham	Glasgow	1805-1869	Brilliant 19th century Scottish chemist, known for Graham's Laws of diffusion/effusion of gases. The word"gel" was coined by him. Responsible for the basic principle of dialysis. (See figure 78)
148	Thomas (Lord Lynedoch)	Graham	Perthshire	1748-1843	British politician and British Army Officer-Lieutenant-General.
149	Kenneth	Grahame	Edinburgh	1859-1932	Author, whose most successful and best-loved children's book is *The Wind in the Willows*. (See figure 79)
150	Katherine	Grainger	Glasgow	1975-	Won numerous titles at the World Rowing Championships. Great Britain's most decorated female Olympian.
151	William	Grant	Dufftown, Grampian	1839-1923	Scottish distiller. Built his own distillery, the Glenfiddich distillery.
152	Alasdair	Gray	Riddrie, East Glasgow	1934-	Scottish writer and artist. His first novel, *Lanark* is now regarded as a classic. He describes himself as a civic nationalist (albeit one deeply critical of English immigration into Scotland) and a republican. (See figure 80)
153	James	Gregory	Aberdeenshire	1638-1675	An astronomer, invented Gregorian telescope. A crater on the moon named after him. (See figure 81)
154	John	Grierson	Kilmadock, Stirlingshire	1898-1972	Scottish documentary film producer.
155	Sir Robert	Grieve	Glasgow	1910-1995	Polymath, engineer, planner, academic, mountaineer, poet, raconteur and visionary.
156	Jo	Grimmond	St Andrews	1913-1993	Scottish Liberal politician. Made a life peer in 1983.
157	Neil	Gunn	Dunbeath	1891-1973	Scottish novelist.
158	Jimmie	Guthrie	Hawick	1897-1937	A motorcycle racer.

No.	First Name	Surname	Birthplace	Born/ Died	Profession/Contribution
159	Thomas	Guthrie	Brechin, Angus	1803-1873	One of the most popular preachers of his day in Scotland and associated with many forms of philanthropy – especially temperance and Ragged Schools, of which he was a founder. (See figure 82)
160	Douglas (1st Earl of Bemersyde)	Haig	Edinburgh	1861-1928	Military leader. Commander in Chief of the British Army in 1915. Founded the Earl Haig Poppy Fund.
161	John	Haldane	Edinburgh	1860-1936	Scottish physiologist. Invented the gas mask during WWI.
162	Iain	Hamilton	Glasgow	1922-2000	Scottish composer.
163	Thomas	Hamilton	Glasgow	1784-1858	Scottish architect. Leading figure in the international Greek Revival. His designs included The Burns Monument Alloway, The Royal College of Physicians of Edinburgh, and the George IV bridge.
164	Sir William	Hamilton	Glasgow	1788-1856	Scottish metaphysician.
165	John	Hannah	East Kilbride	1962-	Film and TV actor.
166	Alan	Hansen	Alloa, Stirlingshire	1955-	Football player and television pundit.
167	James	Harrison	Renton, Dunbartonshire	1816-1893	Engineer, emigrated to Australia. Australian newspaper printer and pioneer in the field of mechanical refrigeration. In Australia, developed the first ever fridge type device in the 1850s.
168	Andrew Gavin	Hastings	Edinburgh	1962-	Rugby Player.
169	Dougal	Haston	Currie, outskirts of Edinburgh	1940-1977	Renowned mountaineer.
170	David	Hayman	Bridgeton, Glasgow	1948-	Scottish film television and stage actor and director.
171	Arthur	Henderson	Glasgow	1863-1935	Labour politician who won the Nobel Peace Prize in 1934.
172	Stephen	Hendry	Auchterarder, Perthshire	1969-	Snooker player, awarded an MBE in 1994, twice voted BBC Scotland's Sports Personality of the Year.
173	David Octavius	Hill	Perth	1802-1870	Scottish painter and arts activist. Produced some of the finest photographic portraits of the 19th century.

No.	First Name	Surname	Birthplace	Born/ Died	Profession/Contribution
174	James	Hogg	Near Ettrick, Selkirkshire	1770-1835	Poet and novelist. A complex, psychologically fragile but uniquely gifted contemporary of Sir Walter Scott.
175	Henry	Home Lord Kames	Berwickshire	1696-1782	Lord Commissioner of High Court of Justiciary and philosopher.
176	Peter	Howson	London	1958-	Scottish painter and war artist.
177	Sir Tom	Hunter	New Cumnock	1961-	Scottish businessman and philanthropist. Knighted in 2005.
178	Sir William	Hunter	Glasgow	1840-1900	Geographer who planned and carried out the first Census of India, in 1872. Scottish historian, statistician, a compiler and a member of the Indian Civil Service. Known for *The Imperial Gazetteer of India*, published in 9 volumes in 1881 and later as a 26 volume set after his death. (See figure 83)
179	Francis	Hutcheson	Born in Ulster	1694-1746	Professor of Moral Philosophy at Glasgow University. Led the way in fresh thinking on moral issues.
180	James	Hutton	Edinburgh	1726-1797	The founder of modern geology. The man who discovered the age of the Earth.
181	Alexander Mackay (Derry)	Irvine	Inverness	1940-	Baron Irvine of Lairg, lawyer, judge and senior political figure.
182	Gordon Cameron	Jackson	Glasgow	1923-1990	Emmy award winning actor best known for the role of the butler, Mr Hudson, in *Upstairs Downstairs*.
183	Michael	Jamieson	Glasgow	1988-	Scottish swimmer. Represented Team GB at the London 2012 Olympics and won the silver medal in the 200 metre breaststroke.
184	Lord Francis	Jeffrey	Edinburgh	1773-1850	Scottish judge and literary critic.
185	John Paul	Jones	Arbigland in Kirkcudbrightshire	1747-1792	Founder of the American navy. Father of the United States Navy.
186	James Norval Herald (James Robertson)	Justice	Lee, a suburb of Lewisham, South London	1907-1975	Journalist and film actor.
187	Lorraine	Kelly	Gorbals, Glasgow	1959-	TV presenter and journalist.

No.	First Name	Surname	Birthplace	Born/Died	Profession/Contribution
188	James	Kelman	Glasgow	1946-	Novelist, playwright, won the Booker Prize in 1994 for *How Late it was, How Late*. Notable for his uncompromising use of idiomatic urban Scots in his work.
189	Sir Ludovic	Kennedy	Edinburgh	1919-2009	Journalist, broadcaster, humanist and author. Also famous for his role in the abolition of the death penalty.
190	Charles	Kennedy	Inverness	1959-2015	Politician and former leader of the Liberal Democratic Party.
191	Helena	Kennedy	Glasgow	1950-	Scottish barrister, writer and broadcaster.
192	Jim	Kerr	Glasgow	1959-	Singer, songwriter and keyboard player.
193	Deborah	Kerr	Helensburgh	1921-2007	Hollywood starlet.(See figure 84)
194	Carole	Kidd	Glasgow	1944-	Scottish jazz singer.
195	Cosmo	Lang	Fyvie, Grampian	1864-1945	Scottish prelate and Archbishop of Canterbury.
196	Sir Harry	Lauder	Portobello	1870-1950	Singer and comedian. (See figure 85)
197	Denis	Law	Aberdeen	1940-	Scottish football player.
198	Andrew Bonar	Law	New Brunswick (now Canada)	1858-1923	Only British Prime Minister to have been born outside the British Isles.
199	Marie MacDonald	Lawrie (LULU)	Lennoxtown, East Dunbartonshire	1948-	Pop singer. Best known for her version of David Bowie's *The Man Who Sold the World*, which Bowie produced.
200	Sir William B	Leishman	Glasgow	1865-1926	Scottish pathologist who helped develop an effective anti-typhoid inoculation. Etiologic agent of Kala-azar named Leishmania.
201	Annie	Lennox	Aberdeen	1954-	Singer and songwriter.
202	Hercules	Linton	Inverbervie, Aberdeenshire	1837-1900	Designed the Cutty Sark, which was built by the firm. Scott and Linton in 1869 on the River Leven in Dumbarton. The fastest tea clipper in the world. (See figure 75)

No.	First Name	Surname	Birthplace	Born/ Died	Profession/Contribution
203	Robert	Liston	Ecclesmachan, West Lothian	1794- 1847	A pioneering Scottish Surgeon. Noted for his skill in an era prior to anaesthetics when speed made a difference in terms of pain and survival.
204	Sir James	Lithgow	Port Glasgow	1883- 1952	Scottish shipbuilder.
205	Liz	Lochhead	Motherwell, Lanarkshire	1947-	Poet, playwright and performer. Edinburgh University awarded her an honorary degree in 2002. Awarded the Queen's Gold Medal for Poetry in 2015.
206	Jimmy	Logan	Dennistoun, Glasgow	1928- 2001	Performer, theatre actor, theatrical producer and impresario.
207	Sir Robert	Lorimer	Edinburgh	1864- 1929	Scottish architect, restored many castles, mansions and churches including Paisley Abbey and Dunblane Cathedral.
208	Sir Charles	Lyell	At Kennedy House Kirriemuir	1797- 1875	Distinguished geologist; conflict between science and religious faith felt throughout his life.
209	Alexander Walter Barr (Sandy)	Lyle	Shrewsbury, England	1958-	Major championship winning golfer.
210	Benny	Lynch	Gorbals, Glasgow	1913- 1946	Boxer. European and World Flyweight Champion.
211	Harry F	Lyte	Native of Ednam near Kelso	1793- 1847	Wrote 'Abide with Me' and other hymns. (See BOXES A & B)
212	Thomas Babington, The Lord	Macaulay	Leicestershire, England	1800- 1859	British historian, introduced English and Western concepts to education in India. Idealised historic British culture and traditions. Rector of the University of Glasgow.
213	Norman	MacCaig	Edinburgh	1910- 1996	Scottish poet awarded Queen's Gold Medal for Poetry in 1985.Original and idiosyncratic, his work displays a lightness of touch rarely found in Scottish poetry.
214	Hugh	MacDiarmid	Langholm, Dumfriesshire	1892- 1978	Nationalist poet, essayist, journalist and political figure. Invented an unwieldy 'Synthetic Scots' idiom intended to advance the cause of Scottish Nationalism.
215	Flora	MacDonald	South Uist	1722- 1790	Jacobite heroine, famous for her part in sheltering Bonnie Prince Charlie. Disguised him as her Irish maid.

No.	First Name	Surname	Birthplace	Born/Died	Profession/Contribution
216	Kelly	Macdonald	Glasgow	1976-	Scottish actress.
217	Sir John Alexander	Macdonald	Glasgow	1815-1891	First Prime Minster of Canada in 1867-1873.
218	Rob Roy	Macgregor	At Glengyle, Loch Katrine	1671-1734	Outlaw and adventurer, participated in the 1715 Jacobite uprising, Folk hero. (See figures 86 A & B)
219	David	Mach	Methill, Fife	1956-	Scottish sculptor.
220	Hamish	MacInnes	Gatehouse of Fleet, Dumfries and Galloway	1930-	Scottish mountaineer, mountain search and rescuer, author and advisor. Invented the MacInnes stretcher used for rescues worldwide.
221	Sir Alexander	Mackenzie	Stornoway, Isle of Lewis	1764-1820	Canadian explorer. The Mackenzie River, the longest in Canada, is named after him.
222	John	Mackenzie	Ross-shire	1839-1901	Emigrated to New Zealand in 1860. Became a politician and served as the Minister of Lands and Agriculture in the Liberal government from 1891-1900.
223	William Lyon	Mackenzie	Dundee	1795-1861	Publisher, journalist and political agitator who led an unsuccessful revolt against the Canadian government in 1837.
224	Sir Compton	Mackenzie	West Hartlepool, County Durham	1883-1972	Author of books such as *Whisky Galore*, Scottish nationalist. His best novel, *Sinister Street*, was admired by F. Scott Fitzgerald, author of *The Great Gatsby*.
225	William	Mackinnon	Campbeltown, Argyll	1823-1893	Founded British India Steam Navigation Company and British East Africa Company.
226	Dougie	MacLean	Perthshire	1954-	Singer/songwriter.
227	Alistair	Maclean	Glasgow	1922-1987	Scottish author. Wrote novels such as *HMS Ulysses* and *The Guns of Navarone*.
228	Sir Fitzroy	MacLean	Cairo, Egypt	1911-1996	Scottish soldier, writer and politician. It is speculated that Ian Fleming used him as the inspiration for James Bond.
229	Sorley	MacLean	Island of Raasay	1911-1996	One of the most significant Scottish poets of the 20th century.
230	John JR	Macleod	Cluny near Dunkeld	1876-1935	Discovered Insulin. Awarded the Nobel Prize for Medicine, which he shared with his co-worker, a research student named Fredrick Banting. (See figure 87)

No.	First Name	Surname	Birthplace	Born/ Died	Profession/Contribution
231	Sir James	MacMillan	Kilwinning, North Ayrshire	1959-	Scottish classical composer and conductor awarded a CBE.
232	Sir Harold	Macmillan	London	1894-1986	British conservative politician, Prime Minister (1957-1963). Educated at Eton and Oxford.
233	Daniel	Macmillan	Isle of Arran	1813-1867	Scottish publisher; founded Macmillan Publishers.
234	Kenneth	Macmillan	Dunfermline	1929-1992	Scottish ballet dancer and choreographer.
235	Lachlan	MacQuarrie	Ulva, off Island of Mull	1762-1824	Governor of New South Wales. Transformed Australia into thriving country, regarded as the Father of Australia.
236	Duncan	Macrae	Maryhill, Glasgow	1905-1967	Leading Scottish stage and screen actor of his generation.
237	Richard	Madden	Elderslie, Renfrewshire	1986-	Scottish stage film and TV actor.
238	Sally	Magnusson	Glasgow	1955-	Broadcaster and writer.
239	Sir Patrick	Manson	Old Meldrum, Aberdeenshire	1844-1922	Regarded as Father of Tropical Medicine. Founder of the original London School of Tropical Medicine.
240	Elizabeth Angela	Marguerite Bowes-Lyon (Queen Elizabeth The Queen Mother)	London	1900-2002	Queen Elizabeth The Queen Mother, The world's favourite gran.
241	Andrew	Marr	Glasgow	1959-	Broadcaster and journalist.
242	Catriona	Matthew	North Berwick	1969-	Scotland's most successful female golfer.
243	Jimmy	Maxton	Pollokshaws, Glasgow	1885-1946	Leader of the Independent Labour Party, conscientious objector and proponent of Scottish home rule.
244	Peter	May	Glasgow	1951-	Scottish TV screenwriter, novelist and crime writer.
245	Sir Robert	McAlpine	Newarthill, Lanarkshire	1847-1934	Scottish building contractor.
246	James	McAvoy	Glasgow	1979-	Scottish stage and screen actor.

No.	First Name	Surname	Birthplace	Born/Died	Profession/Contribution
247	Ian	McCaskill	Glasgow	1938-	Scottish weatherman.
248	Ally	McCoist	Bellshill	1962-	Football player and manager.
249	James Allan (Jim)	McColl	Carmunnock, East Kilbride	1951-	Businessman and entrepreneur.
250	Jim	McColl	Kilmarnock	1935-	Gardener and TV presenter. Best known for presenting The Beechgrove Garden on BBC since 1995. The granddaddy of Scottish horticulture.
251	Ian	McDiarmid	Carnoustie	1944-	Actor and artistic director.
252	William	McEwan	Alloa	1827-1913	Scottish politician and brewer.
253	Ewan	McGregor	Crieff	1971-	Actor, awarded an OBE.
254	William (Willie)	Mcilvanney	Kilmarnock	1936-2015	Scottish novelist, short story writer and poet. Father of the misleadingly named 'Tartan Noir' school of Scottish crime fiction.
255	Lorraine	McIntosh	Cumnock	1964-	Best known as a vocalist with Scottish band Deacon Blue.
256	Kenneth	McKellar	Paisley	1930-2010	Singer. Sang Scotland's traditional songs.
257	Kevin	McKidd	Elgin	1973-	Scottish television and film actor and director.
258	Bill	McLaren	Hawick, Borders	1923-2010	Scottish rugby broadcaster and writer.
259	Henry	McLeish	Methil, Fife	1948-	Scottish Labour politician.
260	Mark	McManus	Hamilton	1936-1994	Actor, best known for his portrayal of DCI Jim Taggart in the long-running TV series Taggart.
261	Colin	McRae	Lanark	1968-2007	Scottish rally driver. Won the world championship in 1995; youngest driver to win the title.
262	Jimmy	McRae	Lanark	1943-	5-time British Rally Champion.
263	Sir David	McVicar	Glasgow	1966-	Directed productions in all the great opera houses around the world. Knighted in 2012.

No.	First Name	Surname	Birthplace	Born/Died	Profession/Contribution
264	Andrew and James (brothers)	Meikle	Houston Mill near Dunbar	Andrew 1719-1811, James 1690-1780	In 1788, invented the threshing machine for removing husks from the grain.
265	Hugh	Miller	Cromarty	1802-1850	Social reformer, political and religious commentator, self-taught expert in geology and folklorist.
266	Michelle	Mone	Glasgow	1971-	Designed Ultimo-bra, huge success. Awarded Peerage in 2015.
267	Arthur	Montford	Glasgow	1929-2014	Sports journalist. Presided over STV's Scotsport for 32 years.
268	Colin Stuart	Montgomerie	Glasgow	1963-	Scottish professional golfer. known for his exceptional performances in the Ryder Cup.
269	Sir John	Moore	Glasgow	1761-1809	The Military General, Lt General, Commander of the great retreat to Corunna. Also commanded at the "Battle of the Pyramids" which decided the fate of Egypt.
270	Edwin	Morgan	Glasgow	1920-2010	Scottish Poet Laureate. In 2004, he was named as the first Scottish national poet: The Scots Makar. Willing to take risks in his work, he experimented with Concrete Poetry, not always successfully.
271	John Lowrie, known as Jolomo	Morrison	Maryhill, Glasgow	1948-	Scottish contemporary artist producing expressionist oil paintings in the Scottish landscapes awarded an OBE.
272	Thomas	Muir	Huntershill, Glasgow	1765-1799	Scottish Political Reformer. Father of Scottish Democracy.
273	Peter	Mullan	Peterhead	1959-	Actor-director.
274	Sir Hugh T	Munro	London	1856-1919	Born into a wealthy Scottish family. Mountaineer and topographer. His name is linked to the summits known as Munros.
275	Donnie	Munro	Uig, Isle of Skye	1953-	Musician performing his unique concerts.
276	Sir Roderick Impey	Murchison	Muir of Ord, Ross-shire	1792-1871	Scottish Geologist who first described and investigated the Silurian System. The crater Murchison on the moon and at least fifteen geographical locations on Earth are named after him.

No.	First Name	Surname	Birthplace	Born/ Died	Profession/Contribution
277	Charles (Chic)	Murray	Greenock	1919-1985	Comedian and entertainer. The first Scottish comedian to use the surreal idiom, Murray was both a stylist and, ironically, a lifelong depressive.
278	Sir James A. H.	Murray	Denholm, in the Borders	1837-1915	Lexicographer. Created the New English Dictionary and edited: A-D, H-K, O-P, and T. Published in 1884 by Oxford University Press.
279	Lord George	Murray	Hunting tower near Perth	1694-1760	Jacobite general.
280	Robert	Napier	Dumbarton	1791-1876	The father of Clyde shipbuilding.
281	James	Nasmyth	Edinburgh	1808-1890	Invented the steam hammer.
282	Alexander	Nasmyth	Grassmarket, Edinburgh	1758-1840	Founder of the landscape school of painting in Scotland.
283	Andrew Ferguson	Neil	Paisley	1949-	Journalist and broadcaster.
284	Graeme	Obree	Nuneaton, Warwickshire, England	1965-	Scottish racing cyclist, nicknamed The Flying Scotsman. Suffers from Bipolar disorder.
285	Sir Alexander	Ogston	Aberdeen	1844-1929	Professor of Surgery at Aberdeen University. Identified the bacterium which he named Staphylococcus aureus. Surgeon to Queen Victoria. Created the Royal Army Medical Corps.
286	Carolina (Lady Nairne)	Oliphant	Gask, Perthshire	1766-1845	Scottish poet and songwriter.
287	Neil	Oliver	Renfrewshire	1967-	TV presenter, author, archaeologist and historian.
288	Lord John Boyd	Orr	Kilmaurs in Ayrshire	1880-1971	First Director General of the United Nations Food and Agriculture Organisation. Awarded a Nobel Prize in 1949.
289	James	Oswald	Glasgow	1779-1853	Merchant. Liberal member of Parliament for Glasgow. Powerful orator, buried in Glasgow Cathedral. (See figure 88)
290	Eduardo Luigi	Paolozzi	Leith	1924-2005	Scottish sculptor and printmaker.
291	Mungo	Park	Fowlsheils, Selkirk	1771-1806	Doctor. Explorer of the river Niger.

No.	First Name	Surname	Birthplace	Born/Died	Profession/Contribution
292	William	Paterson	Tinwald, Dumfriesshire	1658-1719	Scottish financier, founder of the Bank of England.
293	Don	Paterson	Dundee	1963-	Scottish poet, writer and musician.
294	Allan	Pinkerton	Glasgow	1819-1884	Founder of American detective agency.
295	William	Quarrier	Greenock	1829-1903	He pioneered social change in Scotland. A friend of the poor and needy. How one man's determination is still helping so many to this day.
296	Sir Henry	Raeburn	Stockbridge, Edinburgh	1756-1823	Scotland's greatest portrait painter.
297	James Andrew (10th Earl and 1st Marquess of Dalhousie)	Ramsay	Dalhousie Castle, Midlothian	1812-1860	Scottish statesman and a colonial administrator in British India. Governor – General of India (1848-1856).
298	Gordon James	Ramsay	Johnstone, Glasgow	1966-	Celebrity chef and restaurateur.
299	Allan	Ramsay	Edinburgh	1713-1784	Scottish artist. First-rate portrait painter of the 18th century.
300	Ian	Rankin	Cardenden, Fife	1960-	Crime writer. Creator of the Inspector Rebus novels.
301	Jean	Redpath	Edinburgh	1937-	Scottish folk and traditional singer. Internationally renowned as a singer of traditional Scots ballads.
302	James (Jimmy)	Reid	Glasgow	1932-2010	As leader of the Amalgamated Union of Engineering Workers (AUEW) –tried hard to stop government closing Clyde Shipyard; Rector of Glasgow University.
303	Sir Bob	Reid	Cupar, Fife	1934-	Scottish industrial executive, knighted in 1990.
304	John Charles (1st Baron of Stonehaven)	Reith	Stonehaven	1889-1971	Founder, first general manager and Director – General of the BBC, Knighted in 1927. Rector of Glasgow University.
305	John	Rennie	Phantassie, East Lothian	1761-1821	Civil engineer, designer and builder of bridges, roads, canals and aqueducts.
306	Ian	Richardson	Edinburgh	1934-2007	Actor. Awarded a CBE in 2007.
307	Sir John	Richardson	Dumfries	1787-1865	Scottish naturalist and explorer.

No.	First Name	Surname	Birthplace	Born/Died	Profession/Contribution
308	Douglas Argyll	Robertson	Edinburgh	1837-1909	He made several contributions in the field of ophthalmology. Correctly predicted that physostigmine (an extract from Calabar bean) would become very important in the treatment of eye disorders. Described a symptom of neurosyphilis that affects the pupils of the eye, known today as Argyll Robertson pupils. (See figure 89)
309	Rev. William	Robertson	Borthwick, Midlothian	1721-1793	Principal of the University of Edinburgh, historian, minister in the Church of Scotland.
310	Tony	Roper	Glasgow	1941-	Scottish actor, comedian, playwright and writer.
311	Sir Ronald	Ross	Born in India (A Scot by ancestry)	1857-1932	Found the link between mosquitoes and malaria and his work on the breeding grounds of mosquitoes. The man who unravelled the secrets of malaria. Sir Ronald Ross won a Nobel Prize in 1902. (See figure 90)
312	Ricky	Ross	Dundee	1957-	Scottish singer – songwriter and broadcaster. He is the lead singer of the band Deacon Blue.
313	Flora	Sadler	Aberdeen	1912-	Scottish astronomer. First woman scientist to be employed at Royal Observatory, Greenwich.
314	Dougray	Scott	Glenrothes	1965-	Scottish actor.
315	Alexander	Selkirk	Largo in Fife	1676-1721	A seaman who took part in several privateering expeditions. Inspiration for Daniel Defoe's novel *Robinson Crusoe*.
316	Sir James (Jimmy)	Shand	East Wemyss in Fife	1908-2000	Famous accordion player.
317	Bill	Shankly	Glenbuck, Ayrshire	1913-1981	Football player and manager.
318	John	Shepherd-Barron	A Scot born in India	1925-2010	Designed the Cash Machine and four digit PIN number. (See figure 91)
319	Alastair	Sim	Edinburgh	1900-1976	Actor. By far the best female impersonator Scotland has ever produced. His gifts are seen to best effect in the *St Trinians* films of the 1950s.
320	Bill	Simpson	Dunure, Ayrshire	1931-1986	Scottish film and television actor.

No.	First Name	Surname	Birthplace	Born/ Died	Profession/Contribution
321	Sir John	Sinclair	At Thurso Castle, Caithness	1754- 1835	First statistical accounts of Scotland published in 1776. The earliest social survey of its kind. He introduced the word 'statistics' into the English language from German.
322	Sharon	Small	Glasgow	1967-	Actress.
323	Dr William	Smellie	Lanark	1697- 1763	Scottish obstetrician; master of British midwifery.
324	William	Smellie	Edinburgh	1740- 1795	Edited the first edition of "The Encyclopaedia Britannica". (1768-1771).
325	Carol Patricia	Smillie	Glasgow	1961-	TV presenter, actress and former model.
326	Madeleine	Smith	Glasgow	1835- 1928	A 19th century Glasgow socialite who was the accused in a sensational murder trial in Scotland in 1857.
327	Tobias George	Smollet	Renton, Dunbartonshire	1721- 1771	Novelist, first novel *Roderick Random* was popular in 1748; celebrated as "Doctor of Men and Manners" (See figure 92)
328	Dr William Francis	Sommerville	Glasgow		Founded the Girls' Brigade.
329	Mary	Sommerville	Jedburgh, Borders	1780- 1872	Scottish mathematician and astronomer. Supported education and emancipation of women. Sommerville College, Oxford is named after her. Her face will grace the new polymer Royal Bank of Scotland £10 note.
330	Sir Brian Souter and Ann Gloag	Souter & Gloag		Brian Souter, 1954 - Ann Gloag, 1942 -	The Perth based brother and sister team. Stagecoach Transport Group. Brian Souter Knighted in 2011 and Ann Gloag awarded an OBE in 2004.
331	Dame Muriel Sarah	Spark	Edinburgh	1918- 2006	Novelist, best known for *The Prime of Miss Jean Brodie*. On the list of the 50 greatest writers since 1945. A neurotic perfectionist, Spark found writing anything but enjoyable: it is no accident that her novels became shorter and shorter as her career progressed.
332	Catherine Helen	Spence	Melrose	1825- 1910	Scottish-born Australian author, teacher, journalist, politician, leading suffragist.
333	Sir David	Steel	Kirkcaldy, Fife	1938-	Former leader of the Liberal Party. First Presiding Officer of the Scottish Parliament. Awarded knighthood in 1990 and life peerage in 1997.

No.	First Name	Surname	Birthplace	Born/ Died	Profession/Contribution
334	Jock	Stein	Burnbank, Lanarkshire	1922- 1985	Outstanding footballer and manager.
335	Robert	Stevenson	Glasgow	1772- 1850	Lighthouse engineer. Built the Bell Rock Lighthouse in the North Sea in east Scotland in 1811.His son, Thomas, designed and built about 30 lighthouses in Scotland. (See figure 93)
336	Joseph Laughlin (Lachie)	Stewart	Vale of Leven, West Dunbartonshire	1943-	Former Scottish distance runner. Inducted into Scottish Sports Hall of Fame.
337	Andy	Stewart	Glasgow	1933- 1994	Comedian, singer, songwriter and TV personality who was popular on an international scale.
338	Ian	Stewart	Pittenweem, Fife	1938- 1985	One of the founding members of the Rolling Stones, later serving as their road manager and pianist.
339	Professor Dugald	Stewart	Edinburgh	1753- 1826	Scottish philosopher and mathematician.
340	Sir Robert	Stout	Lerwick, Shetland Islands	1884- 1930	Prime Minister of New Zealand.
341	Rev. Robert	Stirling	Galston, Ayrshire	1790- 1878	Manufactured model air engine. 1827. (See figure 94)
342	Sir Archibald David	Stirling	Lecropt, Perthshire	1915- 1990	Mountaineer, WW2 British army officer. Founder of the Special Air service.
343	William	Strang	Dumbarton	1859- 1921	Scottish painter and etcher.
344	Sir James	Swinburne	Inverness	1858- 1958	Scottish scientist and electrical engineer. Pioneer in the plastic industry known as "the father of British plastics". Elected FRS in 1906.
345	Alan	Swinton	Edinburgh	1863- 1930	Scottish electrical engineer and inventor. Elected FRS in 1915.
346	William	Symington	Leadhills, Lanarkshire	1763- 1831	Designed "The Charlotte Dundas", the famous paddle steamer.
347	Archibald	Tait	Edinburgh	1811- 1882	Scottish Anglican prelate and Archbishop of Canterbury.
348	Thomas	Tait	Paisley	1882- 1954	Scottish architect. Chief designer of Glasgow Empire Exhibition of 1938.
349	Robert	Tannahill	Paisley	1774- 1810	Scottish poet of labouring class origin. Known as the Weaver Poet, he wrote dialect lyrics in the wake of Robert Burns.

No.	First Name	Surname	Birthplace	Born/Died	Profession/Contribution
350	David	Tennant	Bathgate	1971-	Scottish film, television and theatre actor. Most famous for his role as 'the tenth doctor' in the BBC science fiction series Dr Who.
351	Sir Charles	Tennant	Laigh Corton, Alloway, Ayrshire	1768-1838	Scottish chemist and industrialist. He discovered bleaching powder.
352	Alexander (Greek)	Thomson	Balfron, Stirlingshire	1817-1875	One of the leading architects in Glasgow in the mid-19th century who designed many important buildings in a late neo-classic style, nearly all of them in the Glasgow area.
353	David	Thomson	Dundee	1861-1954	Scottish newspaper proprietor.
354	Sir Wyville	Thomson	Linlithgow	1830-1882	Scottish oceanographer.
355	Joseph	Thomson	Thornhill, Dumfries and Galloway	1856-1940	Scottish explorer.
356	Rev. John	Thomson of Duddingston	Dailly, Ayrshire	1778-1840	Scottish minister and landscape painter.
357	Archibald	Thorburn	Lasswade, Edinburgh	1860-1935	Scottish bird artist.
358	Sir Alexander	Todd	Glasgow	1907-1997	Unravelled the structure of vitamin B12. Awarded Nobel Prize for Chemistry in 1957. Knighted in 1954. Created Baron Todd in 1962 and made Chancellor of Glasgow University. (See figure 95)
359	Nigel	Tranter	Glasgow	1909-2000	Scottish historian and author.
360	K. T.	Tunstall	St Andrews	1975-	Singer, music style varies from folk to pop.
361	James (Midge)	Ure	Cambuslang, Lanarkshire	1953-	Scottish musician and singer-songwriter. Ure was the lead singer in 1970s Boy Band Slik, and a key figure in the New Romantic school of 1980s pop.
362	Jack	Vettriano	Methil, Fife	1951-	Scotland's most commercially successful artist.
363	Sir James	Walker	Dundee	1863-1935	Scottish physical chemist.

No.	First Name	Surname	Birthplace	Born/Died	Profession/Contribution
364	Kirsty	Wark	Dumfries	1955-	Scottish journalist and television presenter, best known for presenting BBC2's News night since 1993.
365	Jim	Watt	Glasgow	1948-	Boxer. World Lightweight Champion.
366	Willie	Whitelaw	Edinburgh	1918-1999	Scottish Conservative politician. Deputy to Margaret Thatcher, adviser on Falklands War and during general election campaigns. Made Viscount in 1983.
367	Sir David	Wilkie	Cults near Pitlessie in Fife	1785-1841	The artist who portrayed everyday life.
368	Richard	Wilson	Greenock	1936-	Actor, Rector of Glasgow University -1996-1999.
369	James	Wilson	Near St. Andrews	1742-1798	One of the signatories of the American Declaration of Independence. Major force in the drafting of the US Constitution.
370	Charles	Wilson	Edinburgh	1869-1959	Scottish pioneer of atomic and nuclear physics. Shared 1927 Nobel Prize for physics.
371	Alexander	Wilson	Paisley	1766-1813	Author, poet and ornithologist. Published nine volumes of his illustrations of North American birds.
372	Walter	Wingate	Dalry, Ayrshire	1865-1918	Poet, artist.
373	John	Witherspoon	Gifford, East Lothian	1723-1794	Scottish Presbyterian Minister. The only clergyman to sign the American Declaration of Independence. Also signed the Articles of Confederation.
374	Alexander	Wood	Edinburgh	1817-1884	Physician. Invented the hypodermic syringe. (See figure 96)
375	Kirsty Jackson	Young	East Kilbride	1968-	Journalist, TV and radio presenter.

SCOTTISH NOBEL LAUREATES: (1902-2016)

Sir Ronald Ross (1902)
Born in India of Scottish parentage. Awarded the Nobel Prize in Medicine for discovery of the life cycle of malarial parasite.

Sir William Ramsay (1904)
Born in Glasgow. Received the Nobel Prize in Chemistry.

Charles Thomson Rees Wilson (1927)
Born in the parish of Glencarse, Midlothian. Winner of the Nobel Prize in Physics.

John JR MacLeod (1928)
Born in Clunie, near Dunkeld. Awarded a joint Noble Prize in Medicine with Frederick Banting as the co-discoverers of insulin.

Arthur Henderson (1934)
Born in Anderston, Glasgow. Won the Nobel Peace Prize.

Sir Alexander Fleming (1945)
Born at Lochfield farm near Darvel, Ayrshire. Won the Nobel Prize for medicine as a joint award with Howard Florey and Ernst Boris Chain.

John Boyd Orr, 1st Baron Boyd-Orr (1949)
Born in Kilmaurs, Ayrshire. Won the Nobel Peace Prize for advocating a world food policy based on human needs rather than trade interests.

Alexander Robertus Todd, Baron Todd of Trumpington (1957)
Born in Glasgow. Awarded the Nobel Prize for Chemistry.

Sir James Black (1988)
Brought up in Fife. Awarded the Nobel Prize for Medicine.

Sir James Alexander Mirrlees (1996)
Born in Minnigaff, Kirkudbrightshire. He was awarded the Nobel Prize for Economics.

Sir Angus Stewart Deaton (2015)
He was born in Edinburgh. Awarded the Nobel Prize in Economic Sciences for his analysis of Consumption, Poverty and Welfare.

Two scientists born in Scotland won the 2016 Nobel Prize for Physics for their work on storage forms of matter. Professor David Thouless was born in Bearsden and Professor John Kosterlitz is originally from Aberdeen. They shared the award with Professor Duncan Haldane from London for work that "revealed the secrets of exotic matter".

Sir Fraser Stoddart (2016)
A Midlothian farmer's son, the Scottish Chemist won the Nobel Prize for Chemistry. He shared the award with Jean-Pierre Sauvage and Bernard Ferringa for his groundbreaking work on the" design and synthesis of molecular machines".

SECTION B

SOME INTERESTING PHOTOGRAPHS

Figure 69: Electric Pendulum Clock
manufactured by Alexander Bain
*(© The Hunterian, University
of Glasgow 2015)*

Figure 70: The James Braidwood
Memorial Statue in Parliament Square,
Edinburgh

Figure 71(a): A toy
kaleidoscope tube

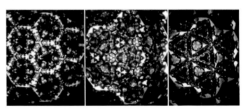

Figure 71 (b): Patterns as seen
through a kaleidoscope

Figure 72: Elgin Marbles in the British Museum

THOMAS CAMPBELL

POET

BORN 1777. DIED 1844.

Figure73: Monument in George Square, Glasgow, to Thomas Campbell the poet

Figure 74: Bonnie Prince Charlie

Figure 75: Cutty Sark at Greenwich before the fire
(Painted by Neil Macleod, Helensburgh, Argyll)

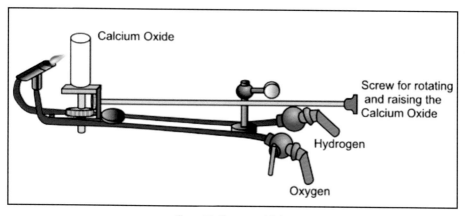

Figure 76: Drummond light

Figure 77: Statue of Robert Fergusson outside the Kirk of the Canongate, Edinburgh

Figure 78: Monument to Thomas Graham (1805-1869), in George Square, Glasgow

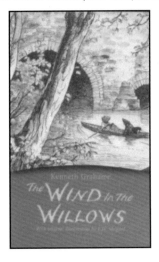

Figure 79: *The Wind in the Willows*

Figure 80: Mural painting by Alasdair Gray on a wall inside The Ubiquitous Chip restaurant, Glasgow
(Photograph: Professor JBP Stephenson, Islay, Argyll)

Figure 81: Gregorian telescope

page **92**

Figure 82: The Statue of Thomas Guthrie on Princes Street, Edinburgh

Figure 83: Imperial Gazetteer of India

Figure 84: Deborah Kerr
(Courtesy Helensburgh Heritage Trust, Helensburgh, Argyll)

Figure 85: Sir Harry Lauder with his famous stick
(By permission of University of Glasgow Library Special Collections)

Box A - Abide With Me

- 'Abide with Me' is a Christian hymn by Scottish Anglican Henry Francis Lyte.
- Lyte wrote it in 1847 while he lay dying from tuberculosis; he survived only a further three weeks after its completion.
- The hymn is a prayer to GOD: throughout life, through trials, and through death.
- The hymn tune most often used is "Eventide" by William Henry Monk.
- The hymn was said to be a favourite of King George V and Mahatma Gandhi.
- The hymn is sung at Military Services and Remembrance Day services in the United Kingdom.
- The first and last verses of the hymn are traditionally sung at the FA Cup Final before the kick-off of the match.
- The hymn has been sung prior to the kick-off at every Rugby League Challenge Cup final since 1929, the first final to be held at Wembley Stadium.
- Abide with Me was sung at the 2012 Summer Olympics Ceremony.

Box B - Abide With Me by Henry Francis Lyte (1793-1847)

1. Abide with me;
   fast falls the eventide;
   the darkness deepens;
   Lord, with me abide;
   when other helpers fail,
   and comforts flee,
   help of the helpless,
   O abide with me.

2. Swift to its close
   ebbs out life's little day;
   earth's joys grown dim,
   its glories pass away;
   change and decay
   in all around I see;
   O thou who changest not,
   abide with me.

3. I need thy presence
   every passing hour;
   what but thy grace can foil
   the tempter's power?
   Who like thyself my guide
   and stay can be?
   Through cloud and sunshine,
   Lord, abide with me.

4. I fear no foe
   with thee at hand to bless;
   ills have no weight,
   and tears no bitterness.
   Where is death's sting?
   where, grave, thy victory?
   I triumph still,
   if thou abide with me.

5. Hold thou thy cross
   before my closing eyes,
   shine through the gloom,
   and point me to the skies;
   heaven's morning breaks,
   and earth's vain shadows flee;
   in life, in death, O Lord,
   abide with me.

Figure 86(a): Rob Roy Macgregor

Figure 86(B): The Clachan Oak, on the green in Balfron, Stirlingshire is thought to date from 1533. Known locally as the hanging tree, it is said that Rob Roy MacGregor hid there in 1711 while on the run from the Duke of Montrose. The tree is notable for the two large iron hoops that now hold the hollow trunk together.

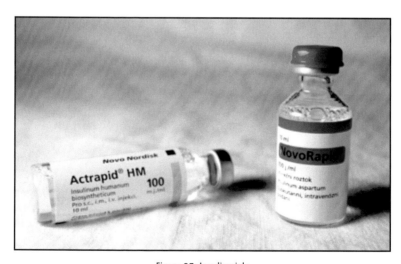

Figure 87: Insulin vials

Figure 88: Monument to James Oswald (1779-1853) in George Square Glasgow

Figure 89: Douglas Argyll Robertson *(Reproduced Courtesy of Royal College of Physicians and Surgeons of Glasgow)*

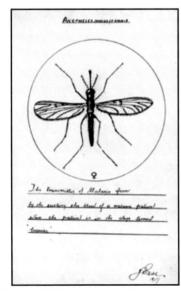

Figure 90: Link between mosquito and malaria
(Reproduced courtesy of Royal College of Physicians and Surgeons of Glasgow)

Figure 91: Cash Machine and 4 digit Pin number designed by John Shepherd-Barron

Figure 92: Tobias Smollett
(Courtesy Dumbarton Library, Dumbarton)

Figure 93: Bell Rock lighthouse, Arbroath
(Courtesy of Angus Archives, Copyright Angus Council)

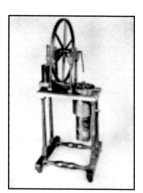

Figure: 94:
Robert Stirling's Model Air Engine
(© The Hunterian, University of Glasgow 2015)

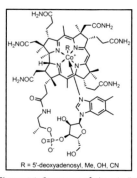

R = 5'-deoxyadenosyl, Me, OH, CN

Figure 95: Structure of vitamin B12

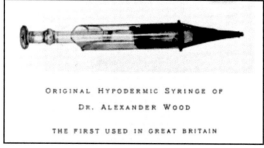

ORIGINAL HYPODERMIC SYRINGE OF

DR. ALEXANDER WOOD

THE FIRST USED IN GREAT BRITAIN

Figure 96: Hypodermic syringe
(Courtesy Wellcome Images Library, London)

SCOTTISH WWI HEROINES

Scottish heroines who served in Serbia during the First World War are being honoured on a stamp collection in Serbia. Serbia was desperate for medical assistance during the war. Britain sent about 600 women to serve as doctors, nurses and drivers. The British Embassy in Serbia worked with the Serbia Post to recognise the women involved and create the stamps.

Those featured include Dr Elsie Inglis (born in India: 1864-1917) —one of the first female graduates of the University of Edinburgh – who founded the Scottish Women's hospitals project in Serbia. The organisation was set up in Edinburgh but moved to battlefields across Europe to help the war effort and promote women's rights. (Also see Section A, 31)

Other Scottish doctors honoured on the stamps include Surgeon Dr Katherine MacPhail (1887 – 1974) who opened the first paediatric ward in Belgrade in 1921. Katherine MacPhail spent much of her adult life in Serbia and continues to be remembered there for the contribution she made to orthopaedic surgery. After the war Katherine remained in Serbia, running her own small hospital the Anglo – Serbian Children's Hospital in Belgrade. In 1934 she established the English – Yugoslav Hospital for Treatment of Osteoarticular Tuberculosis in Sremska Kamenica. Her war work had been honoured by the Serbian government, which conferred the Serbian Order of St Sava and Serbian Red Cross. Her peacetime work was recognised in 1928, when she was awarded the OBE. Katherine MacPhail, a heroine in war and peace, died in 1974.

Dr Isabel Emslie Galloway Hutton, CBE (born in Edinburgh: 1887 – 1960) was a Scottish medical doctor who specialised in mental health and social work. She joined Scottish Women's Hospitals as a volunteer in 1915 after she was turned away by the War office in London. Dr Hutton served in France, Greece and Serbia.

The stamps also honour Evelina Haverfield (born at Inverlochy Castle, Kingussie: 1867 – 1920), who was chief administrator of Scottish Women's Hospitals in Serbia, where she set up one of the country's first orphanages. Ms Haverfield was awarded the highest state honours. She died in 1920 of pneumonia in Serbia, having gone there to work in an orphanage.

Dr Elizabeth Ross (born in Tain: 1878 – 1915) was one of the first women to obtain a medical degree at the University of Glasgow. She travelled to Serbia as a volunteer and sadly passed away during the typhoid epidemic in 1915 in a military hospital in Kragujevac where she had been treating First World War casualties.

Captain Flora Sandes (originally from Yorkshire: 1876 – 1956) was the only British woman to bear arms in the First World War, as she became an officer in the Serbian Army. She was awarded the highest medal for her role.

The British Embassy in Serbia has partnered up with the Serbia Post to launch a series of stamps commemorating British Heroines of WW1. As well as remembering their services to the War, the Embassy's campaign has been highlighting the values of these women (such as universal suffrage, solidarity, social and gender equality to help build strong relationships with leaders and communities in Serbia).

The stamps were launched in December, 2015, featuring six iconic women – Flora Sandes, Evelina Haverfield, Dr Elsie Inglis, Dr Katherine MacPhail, Dr Emslie Hutton whose War efforts are still celebrated in communities across Serbia (See figures 97 (a), (b), (c) & (d): (Courtesy of Foreign & Commonwealth Office, London).

Figure 97 (a): Series of six stamps (L to R: Top row: Flora Sandes, Dr Katherine McPhail, Dr Elsie Inglis, Bottom row: Dr Isabel Emslie Hutton, Evelina Haverfield, Dr Elizabeth Ross)

(Courtesy of Foreign and Commonwealth Office, London)

Figure 97 (b): Dr Isabel Emslie Hutton, Dr Elsie Inglis *(Courtesy of Foreign and Commonwealth Office, London)*

Figure 97 (c): Evelina Haverfield, Dr Elizabeth Ross *(Courtesy of Foreign and Commonwealth Office, London)*

Figure 97 (d): Flora Sandes, Dr Katherine MacPhail *(Courtesy of Foreign and Commonwealth Office, London)*

SCOTTISH PAINTERS

(a) THE GLASGOW 'BOYS' (In 1880s)

The Glasgow Boys were a gifted group of artists; painting in Britain at the end of the 19th century. They were linked by connections with Glasgow, where they lived, studied or had their studios.

At first they painted rural people and landscapes. Later they depicted the inhabitants of Glasgow's affluent suburbs. Travel and street life also inspired the Glasgow Boys. Interestingly, Japanese motifs can be seen in Glasgow Boys work because they regarded Japan as a model society and aimed to reflect this in their paintings. A number of them also became successful portrait painters.

THE GLASGOW BOYS ARE SOME OF SCOTLAND'S BEST-LOVED ARTISTS.

They enjoyed national and international fame. The following are generally considered 'The Glasgow Boys':

- Joseph Crawhall, born in Morpeth, but moved to Glasgow to continue his studies. Guthrie, Walton and Crawhall worked together at Roseneath and Brig o' Turk. (1861-1913)
- Thomas Millie Dow, born Dysart, Fife. In addition to painting landscapes and figures in landscapes, Dow was also a notable flower painter. (1848-1919)
- David Gauld, born Glasgow, his reputation was established with his painting of cattle and calves in landscapes. (1867-1936) (See figure 98)
- Sir James Guthrie, born Greenock, a leading portrait painter. Became President of RSA. (1859-1930) (See figure 99)
- James Whitelaw Hamilton, born Glasgow. His best work is of fishing villages with people gathered on the quays. (1860-1932)
- George Henry, born Ayrshire. In 1893, Henry and Hornel set off for Japan. During their nineteen months there, both Henry and Hornel produced some of their finest work. Henry's Japanese period is principally represented by watercolours. (1858-1943)
- Edward Atkinson Hornel, born Bacchus Marsh, New South Wales, and moved to Scotland with his parents to settle at Kirkcudbright in 1866. He painted children in fancy dress, figures in flower-decked woods, autumnal forests and flowers and girls by the sea. An exhibition of his Japanese works held in Glasgow was a success. (1864-1933) (See figure 100)

- William Kennedy, born Hutchesontown, Glasgow, and studied in Paris. Kennedy painted many rural scenes, showing harvesters, children playing in fields and woods, and evening scenes in the country. (1859-1918)
- Sir John Lavery, born in Belfast. He studied at the Haldane Academy in Glasgow. Lavery was well established as a portrait painter and also painted landscapes in Scotland. One of the most interesting artists of his period. (1856-1941)
- Alexander Mann, born Glasgow, he painted landscape scenes, with figures playing a smaller role. (1853-1908)
- Charles Hodge Mackie. Born in Aldershot, he was brought up in Edinburgh and studied at RSA Schools. He produced a number of bold watercolours as well as some interesting wood block prints. He had a large circle of artistic friends in Edinburgh. (1862-1920)
- Thomas McEwan. Born near Glasgow, he produced a large number of genre and historical works, mostly painted in watercolour. (1846-1914)
- Bessie McNicol (Mrs Alexander Frew). Born in Glasgow, she produced portraits and sensitive maternity scenes influenced by Guthrie, Henry, and Hornel. (1869-1904)
- William York Macgregor. Born Finnart, Dunbartonshire, the son of a Glasgow shipbuilder. He was known as the 'father of the GLASGOW BOYS'. He painted oils, often of hilly landscapes with rock faces or quarries, using thickly applied paint. (1855-1923)
- Arthur Melville. Born in Angus, some of his most sparkling watercolours are of Eastern subjects. Melville is the greatest water-colourist of his period. (1855-1904)
- James Paterson. Born Glasgow, Paterson painted the landscape around Moniaive in Dumfriesshire in oil and watercolour. Unlike many of the other Glasgow Boys, Paterson's later work does not decline in quality. (1854-1932) (See figure 101)
- John Quinton Pringle, born in the east end of Glasgow. Pringle was greatly admired by other artists, despite his modest output. His best work, such as Poultry Yard, Whalsay Bay with Girl in White, has a haunting quality. (1864-1925)
- Alexander Roche. Born Glasgow, he painted a number of rather romantic pictures of girls in gardens, interiors or in landscape. He was particularly good at portraits of women. (1861-1921)
- Edward Arthur Walton, born at Glanderston House, Renfrewshire. He made a remarkable series of watercolours in Helensburgh in 1883 depicting the prosperous suburb and its well-dressed people. These watercolours are amongst the finest of the Glasgow School with their clarity of image and colour. (1860-1922)
- Macaulay Stevenson. Born Glasgow, he was a fine water-colourist; he had the ability to capture rivers seen at dusk or in moonlight. (1854-1952)

Closely associated with the Glasgow School at various times were J.E. Christie, born in Fife, (1847-1914); J.S. Park, born Kilmarnock, Ayrshire,(1862-1933) and Sir George Pirie, born Campbeltown,(1866-1940).

Figure 98: David Gauld, Music, oil,
(© The Hunterian, University of Glasgow 2015)

Figure 99: Gravestone of Sir James Guthrie at Rhu & Shandon Parish Church, Argyll

Figure 100: Edward Atkinson Hornel: "Brig House Bay"
(Courtesy Paisley Museum, Renfrewshire Council)

Figure101: James Paterson, Moniaive, oil,
(© The Hunterian, University of Glasgow 2015)

(b) THE NEW GLASGOW 'BOYS' (1983 - 1997)

The New Glasgow Boys (Steven Campbell, Ken Currie, Peter Howson and Adrian Wiszniewski) studied at The Glasgow school of Art in the 1980s and achieved national and international success for renewing interest in the painting of the human figure at a time when American abstract, pop and conceptual art dominated Western art. The success of this group was an important factor in Glasgow's recent cultural renaissance.

(c) SCOTTISH COLOURISTS

The Scottish Colourists were a group of post-impressionist artists:

- Samuel John Peploe. Born Edinburgh, best known for his still lifes of roses or tulips. Peploe had a wide range of subjects including figure painting and, particularly, landscape. (1871-1935) (See figure 102)
- Francis Cadell. Born Edinburgh, his work showed a tendency towards clear-cut still lifes and interior scenes with an emphasis on the creation of precise, almost geometric patterns. (1883-1937)
- Leslie Hunter. Born Rothesay. His work is never repetitive; he appears to be constantly searching, through his drawings, for a new approach. (1879-1931)
- J.D. Fergusson. Born Leith. Fergusson was one of the most versatile of the Colourists. He was an excellent draughtsman as his style and, in particular, his often witty Parisian watercolours reveal. (1874-1961)

They blended Scottish painting traditions with the influence of French artists such as Monet and Cézanne. They must be considered a seminal influence on the development of Scottish art in the 20th century. Their works can be seen in various Scottish galleries.

Figure 102: Samuel John Peploe, 'Tulips in a Vase', oil,
(© The Hunterian, University of Glasgow 2015

SCOTTISH PLANT HUNTERS

Scotland has over the last two centuries or so produced some of the world's most successful plant hunters. The plant hunters were not just botanists; they were adventurers and explorers. They approached the unknown to find, and bring back for cultivation, a vast number of new and exotic plants. The Scottish Plant Hunters' Garden beside the Festival Theatre in Pitlochry, Perthshire, aims to show in a natural setting many of these plants. There were over 120 plant hunters of Scottish descent. Here just thirteen of the plant hunters are mentioned.

1: David Douglas: Year of Birth - 1799
   • Born in Scone, Perthshire.
   • He worked in the Botanic Gardens in Glasgow and the Horticultural Society of London
   • Between 1824-1827 he collected the seeds of many coniferous trees, including the Douglas fir (Pseudotsuga menziesii and the Sika spruce (Picea sitchensis), the flowering currant (Ribes sanguineum) and California poppy (Eschscholzia californica).
   • Although the common name Douglas-fir refers to him the tree's scientific name honours a rival botanist Archibald Menzies. However, many species of plants have douglasii in their scientific names in his honour.
   • He laid claim to introducing over 200 new species.
   • One of the greatest plant hunters of all time.

> David Douglas:
> Plants introduced into Britain:
> Douglas's major discoveries were conifers; he also found several lovely shrubs.
> Douglas fir ((Pseudotsuga menziesii), Phlox, Penstemon, Clarkia, Lupinus polyphyllus, Mimulus, Rose of Sharon, Hypericum, Gaillardia, Mahonia, Ceanothus, Geranium, Heuchera, Lathyrus (Sweet pea), Potentilla, Viola, Spiraea, Abies grandis (Grand fir), Abies procera (Noble fir), Pinus radiata (Monterey pine), Garrya elliptica, Ribes sanguineum (Flowering currant). (See figures 103 and 104)

Figure103: Douglas fir (Pseudotsuga menziesii)

Figure104: Garrya elliptica
(Courtesy the Hardy Plant Society)

page 108

2: James Drummond: Year of Birth - 1786
- Born in Inverarity, near Forfar.
- Started work as an employee of George Dickson in Edinburgh, nurseryman.

James Drummond:
Plants introduced into Britain;
Dasypogon hookerii(a plant of botanical but not of horticultural importance), Black flowered Boronia megastigma, Banksias, Dryandras, Anigozanthus pulcherrinus, Backhausia myrtifola, Leschendaultia lacina, Chorizema varium, Pimelia spectabilis, Leschenaultia biloba, Acacia drummondi was named after him. (See figure 105)

Figure 105: Banksia ericifolia
(Courtesy the Hardy Plant Society)

3: John Fraser: Year of Birth - 1750
- Born during the Age of Enlightenment at Tomnacross, the Aird, Inverness-shire
- Botanist and plant collector.

John Fraser:
Plants introduced into Britain:
Varieties of Rhododendron and hydrangea, Phlox stolonifera (Creeping Phlox), Magnolia fraseri. Fraser was the first European to collect Rhododendron catawbiense.

4: George Forrest: Year of Birth - 1873
  • Born in Falkirk.
  • He worked in the herbarium at the Botanic Gardens, Edinburgh.

George Forrest:
Plants introduced into Britain:
Primula bulleyana, Primula vialii, Gentian sino-ornata, Rhododendron haematodes, Rhododendron sinogrande, Camellia reticulata, Camellia saluensis, Rhdodendron griersonianum, and Magnolia campbelii, Abies forestii, Cotoneaster lacteus, Daphne auraantiaca, Hypericum forestii, Iris chrysographes, Jasminum polyanthum, Pieris Formosa var forestii, Primula aurantiaca, Primula melanops, Osmanthus yunnanensis (See figure 106)

Figure 106: Magnolia campbelli
(Courtesy the Hardy Plant Society)

5: Robert Fortune: Year of Birth - 1812
  • Born in Edrom, near Dun in the Scottish Borders.
  • Served an apprenticeship in the garden of Kelloe.
  • Worked at the Royal Botanic Garden, Edinburgh. Became superintendent of the indoor plant section of the Horticulture Society Garden at Chiswick London.
  • Appointed to the position of Society's Plant Collector in China.
  • He went on plant-hunting excursions into north China to collect seeds and plants of ornamental value not already cultivated in Britain.
  • During his time in China Fortune dressed as a Chinaman, with shaved head and pigtail and became fluent in Mandarin. By shaving his head and adopting a ponytail he effectively blended into the crowd and was able to enter the strictly forbidden cities unnoticed.

- In 1848 on behalf of the East India Company he collected tea plants (Camellia sinensis) and took these tea plants to India. Thus Fortune was responsible for laying the foundation of tea trade in India under the control of the British traders.

> Robert Fortune:
> Plants introduced into Britain:
> Cryptomeria japonica, Anemone japonica, Forsythia var fortunei, Jasminum nudiflorum, Weigela florida, Mahonia japonica, Rhododendron fortunei, Dicentra spectabilis, Primula japonica, Chrysanthemum pompon section, Deutzia scabra, Azalea sp, Rododendron sp, Forsythia and Jasminum officinale, Palm trees: Trachycarpus fortunei (See figures 107 and 108)

Figure107: Lamprocapnos spectabilis
(formerly Dicentra spectabilis)
(Courtesy the Hardy Plant Society)

Figure 108: Tea plantation in Darjeeling, India
(Photograph: Nigel Allan, Helensburgh, Argyll)

6: Sir Joseph Hooker: Year of Birth - 1817
- Born in Halesworth, Suffolk.
- His father, Sir William Hooker (1785-1865) was director of Kew Gardens.
- Spent his childhood in Glasgow. Attended Glasgow High School.
- Studied medicine at Glasgow University.
- Became Director of The Royal Botanic Gardens at Kew.
- Recognised as the most important botanist of the 19th century.
- His major published work is the seven-volume Flora of British India (1872-1897).
- Collected 30 new species of Rhododendron – described in his magnificent book, Rhododendron of the Sikkim-Himalaya.
- Was President of the Royal Society (1873-1878) and received a knighthood in 1877.

Sir Joseph Hooker:
Plants introduced into Britain:
Primula capitata, Primula sikkimensis, Introduced Himalayan rhododendrons, between 1849-1851, Rhododendron cinnabarinum, Rhododendron falconeri, Rhododendron griffithianum, Rhododendron hodgsonii, Rhododendron thomsonii. (See figures 109 and 110)

Figure 109: Rhododendron thomsonii
(Courtesy Fiona Devlin, Tarbert, Argyll)

Figure 110: Rhododendron falconeri
(Courtesy Fiona Devlin, Tarbert, Argyll)

7: David Lyall: Year of Birth - 1817
- Studied medicine in Aberdeen.
- A naval surgeon – as assistant surgeon he had to make botanical collections.

David Lyall:
Plants introduced into Britain:
Hebe elliptica, Hebe speciosa, Ranunculus lyallii (Butter cup), Arabis lyallii, Larix lyallii, the sub-alpine Larch, Anemone lyallii, Astelia nervosa, Fuchsia procumbens, Pittosporum tenufolium

8: Francis Masson: Year of Birth - 1741
   • Born in Aberdeen.
   • Gardener at the royal gardens at Kew in London.
   • Accompanied Captain Cook on his second circumnavigation in 1772.

> Francis Masson:
> Plants introduced into Britain:
> Pelargonium(introduced some 50 species of Pelargonium), Lobelia, Gladioli sp,Ixia spTrillium grandiflora (Trinity flower), White arum lily (Zantedeschia aethiopica), Kniphofia, Amaryllis belladonna, Nerine sarniensis(valued for their funnel-shaped lily-like flowers). (See figures 111, 112 and 113)

Figure111:
White Arum Lily
(Zantedeschia aethiopica)

Figure112: Kniphofia (Red hot poker)

Figure113: Amaryllis belladonna
(Courtesy the Hardy Plant Society)

9: Archibald Menzies: Year of Birth - 1754
   • Graduated in medicine at Edinburgh University.
   • Worked in the garden of Castle Menzies.

> Archibald Menzies:
> Plants introduced into Britain
> Monkey puzzle tree (Araucaria araucana) from Chile, Banksias, Mock orange - Philadelphus, funny slipper orchid, Mahonia acquifolium, Rhododendron occidentalis, Arbutus menzesii, Thuja plicata (Red cedar) Cornus nuttalii (Pacific Dogwood), Cupressus nootkatensis, Quercus garryana, Quercus lobata, Spiraea douglasii var menziesii (See figure 114)

Figure114: Monkey Puzzle tree
(Araucaria araucana) from Chile

10: George Sherriff: Year of Birth - 1898
  - Born in Larbert.
  - Educated at Sedbergh and the Royal Military Academy, Woolwich.

George Sherriff:
Plants introduced into Britain:
Primula ludlowii, Primula sherriffii, Mecnopsis sherriffii, Abies spectabilis, Berberis sherriffii, Bergenia ligulata, Euphorbia griffithii, Paenoia lutea and others.

11: Thomas Thomson: Year of Birth - 1817
  - Born in Glasgow.
  - Graduated in medicine.
  - In 1854 he took charge of Calcutta Botanic Garden and held the Chair of Botany at Calcutta Medical College, India (now Kolkata, India).

Figure 115: Rhododendron thomsonii
(Courtesy Fiona Devlin, Tarbert, Argyll)

Thomas Thomson:
Plants introduced into Britain:
Rhododendron thomsonii, Rhododendron falconeri, Rhododendron sinogrande, Abies spectabilis, Cedrus deodara, Primula denticulata, Primula rosea, Prunus armenaica, Anemone pratensis, Asphodelus pyramidalis,Fritillaria imperialis (See figure 115)

12: Euan Cox, Peter Cox, Kenneth Cox
  - Three generations of plant hunting dynasty of Glendoick Garden Centre, Glencarse, Perthshire-1919 to the present.
  - Some of the most notable rhododendrons introduced since 1981.

Euan Cox, Peter Cox, Kenneth Cox
Plant introductions into Britain:
Rhododendron dendrachasis, Rhododendron ochraceum, Rhododendron platypodum, Rhododendron denudatum, Rhododendron trilectorum, Rhododendron luciforum, Rhododendron monanthum, Rhododendron huianum, Rododendron laudandum, Rhododendron dignabile and others.

13: George Don: Year of Birth – 1798
  • Don worked in his father's nursery gardens, Edinburgh.

George Don
Plant introductions into Britain:
Allium sp, Erythronium americanum, Acquilegia canadensis, Iris foetidissima, Kalamia latifolia, Hamamelis virginica, Rhododendron sp, Aralia spinosa

SECTION F

SCOTLAND THE PIONEER

1: The Game of Golf:
    - The exact origins of the sport of golf are unclear. The most widely accepted theory is that the modern game of golf originated in Scotland in the High Middle Ages.
    - Golf has been played at the legendary Old Course at St Andrews since the 15th century and in 1759 it became the first course in the world to have eighteen holes.
    - The first written rules for playing golf originated in Scotland.
    - Scotland has 578 golf courses, which are divided among its ten regions. The highest concentrations are around Glasgow (94 courses) and Edinburgh (67 courses).
    - The modern game was spread by Scots to the rest of the world.
      (See figure 116)

2: Dolly the Cloned Sheep
    - In 1997, a research team based at the Roslin Institute in Midlothian created Dolly the Sheep, the world's first cloned mammal, and caused a worldwide sensation. The research was directed by a non-Scot, Dr Ian Wilmut, but came into existence in Scotland. Dolly was the first clone derived from skin cells genetically altered. A clone is an organism is genetically identical to its parent and the result of asexual reproduction.
    - Dolly died of arthritis early in 2003, at the age of six years. (See figure 117)

Figure116: The Carrick Golf Club, Loch Lomond, Argyll

Figure 117: Dolly the Cloned Sheep

SCOTTISH NATIONAL PORTRAIT GALLERY, EDINBURGH

The Scottish National Portrait Gallery in Queen Street, Edinburgh, opened in 1889, and has a frieze which goes round the Great Hall of the Gallery below the first-floor balustrade. It was created by the artist William Brassey Hole in 1898 and depicts 155 men and women deemed in the late 19th century the greatest in Scottish history. The figures shown are in chronological sequence (running backwards in time). Also the images here overlap to a certain extent in order to ensure that all the historical characters are included. (See figures 118: a, b, c & d): *(Courtesy Scottish National Portrait Gallery, Edinburgh)*.

Figure 118 (a)

Figure 118 (b)

Figure 118 (c)

Figure 118 (d)

ACKNOWLEDGEMENTS

The author is extremely grateful to Angus Archives (Angus Council), Clydesdale Bank, The Royal Bank of Scotland, Bank of Scotland, Dumbarton Library, Dumbarton, Glasgow Museums, Paisley Museum, Helensburgh Heritage Trust, The Hunterian-University of Glasgow, University of Glasgow Library, Special Collections, Royal College of Physicians & Surgeons of Glasgow, Royal College of Physicians of Edinburgh and Wikipedia-The Free Encyclopedia and others for giving permission to reproduce some of the images from their collection free of charge. Also the author gratefully acknowledges the help of the many people who willingly provided photographs for this publication, and others for their constructive suggestions. Without their invaluable help it would have been impossible to produce an illustrated book.

Finally, I would like to acknowledge the considerable creative and editorial contribution made to the text by Dr John Murie MA; MEd; PhD.